An Invitation To Know Him

For Yourself

by

Mamie D. Givhan

authorHOUSE®

AuthorHouse™
1663 Liberty Drive
Bloomington, IN 47403
www.authorhouse.com
Phone: 1-800-839-8640

Published by AuthorHouse 4/21/2012

ISBN: 978-1-4343-1896-1 (sc)
ISBN: 978-1-4670-9288-3 (e)

INTRODUCTION

This course consists of the first five books of the Old Testament and the first five books of the New Testament. It is set in chronological order, (by chapters and verses thereby noting the summary of events in historical order). This invitation to know Him for yourself is developed to aid you in reading your Bible, gaining insight, retaining detailed information, and defining your purpose and plans to promote the Word of God. This course corresponds with the King James Version Bible.

In reading your Bible, you will gain insight through deeper consecration by completing each blank during or after reading. This method presents a challenge to you, and by following through, personal satisfaction is accomplished.

The retaining of this information is very important—for it will not change. When you encounter any selected verse from these 10 books, regardless of how it is presented, or from any perspective, you will know the story and will magnify God even more. Following these lessons, the essays have the answers to the questions, to see that your answers coincide with the Bible.

I believe that each individual has a divine purpose and plan in his or her life; hence, *Before I formed thee in the belly, I knew thee...*(Jeremiah 1:5). Therefore, I believe you can find your divine purpose and plan through the Word of God. Stay in a good Bible-based church.

THE OLD TESTAMENT

GENESIS

1. In the beginning _____ created the heaven and the earth.

2. And the earth was without form, and void; and darkness was upon the face of the deep. _____ _____ _____ _____ _____

_____ _____ _____ _____ _____ _____

_____.

3. And God called the light _____ and the darkness he called _____ and the evening and the morning were the _____ _____.

4. And God called the firmament _____. And the evening and the morning were the _____ _____.

5. And God said, let there be lights in the firmament of the heaven to divide the day from the night; _____ _____ _____ ____ _____

_____, _____ _____ _____ _____ _____

_____ _____ _____.

6. So God created man in his own image, in the image of _____ created he him; _____ _____ _____ _____

_____ _____.

7. On the seventh day God ended his work which he had made; and he rested on the seventh day from all his work which he had made. And God _____

_____ _____ _____, _____ _____

_____: because that in it he had rested from all his work which God created and made.

8. And the Lord God formed man of the dust of the   ground, and _____

_____ _____ _____ _____ _____

_____ _____ _____ _____ _____ ____

_____ _____ .

9. And the Lord God caused a deep sleep to fall upon Adams, and he slept:
_____ _____ _____ _____ ____ _____ ____ , and
closed up the flesh instead thereof. And the rib, _____ _____

_____ _____ _____ _____ , _____

_____ _____ _____ ____ _____ , and brought her unto the man.

And Adam said, _____ _____ _____ _____ _____

_____ _____ _____ _____ _____ _____

_____ :   she shall be called woman, because she was taken out of
man. Therefore shall a man leave his father and his mother and shall cleave unto
his wife _____ _____ _____ ____ _____ _____

And they were both naked, the man and his wife, and _____ _____

_____ .

10. And the serpent said unto the woman, ye shall _____ surely die.

11. And the Lord God said unto the serpent, because thou hast done this ____

_____ _____ above all cattle, and above every beast of the field;

_____ _____ _____ _____ ,

_____ _____ _____ _____ _____

_____ _____ _____ _____ _____

_____ .

12. Unto Adam also and to his wife did the Lord God make coats of skins
_____ _____ _____ .

13. And Adam knew Eve his wife ; _____ _____ _____

_____ _____ _____ , and said, I have gotten a man
from the Lord. And she again bare his brother _____ . And Abel was a

_____ _____ _____, but Cain was a _____

_____ _____ _____.

14. And Cain talked with Abel his brother; and it came to pass, when they were in the field, _____ _____ _____ _____ _____

_____ _____ _____, _____

_____ _____.

15. And Cain said unto the Lord, _____ _____ _____

_____ _____ _____ _____ _____.

16. And Cain knew his wife; and she conceived _____ _____

_____: and he built a city, and called the name of the city, _____

_____ _____ _____ _____ _____,

_____.

17. And Adam lived an hundred and thirty years, and begat a son in his own likeness, after his image, _____ _____ _____ _____

_____.

18. And Lamech lived an hundred eighty and two years, and _____ ____

_____; and he called his name _____, saying, this same shall comfort us concerning our work and toil of our hands _____

_____ _____ _____ _____ _____

_____ _____ _____ _____.

19. And Noah was five hundred years old: and Noah begat _____,

_____, _____ _____.

20. That the sons of God saw the daughters of men that they were fair; _____

_____ _____ _____ _____ _____

_____ _____ _____ _____.

21. And God saw that _____ _____ ____ _____

_____ _____ _____ _____ _____ , and that

every imagination of the thoughts of his heart was _____ _____

_____.

22. But Noah found _____ _____ _____ _____

_____ _____ _____.

23. And God said to Noah, _____ _____ _____ _____

_____ ____ _____ _____ _____;

for the earth is filled with violence through them, and, behold, ____ ____

_____ _____ _____ _____ _____

_____.

24. And, behold, I, even I, do _____ ___ _____

_____ _____ _____ _____ _____ _____

_____ _____ _____ _____ _____ ____

_____ _____ _____.

25. But with thee will I establish my covenant; _____ _____

_____ _____ _____ _____ _____ , thou

and thy sons, and thy wife, and thy sons' wife with thee.

26. Thus did Noah; according to all that God commanded him, _____

_____ _____.

27. In the six hundredth year of Noah's life, _____ _____ _____

_____ , _____ _____ _____

_____ _____ _____ , the same day were all the fountains

of the great deep broken up, and the _____ _____

_____ _____ _____. And the rain was upon

4

the earth _____ _____ _____ _____

_____.

28. And the water prevailed upon the earth an _____

_____ _____ _____.

29. And the dove came in to him in the evening; and lo, in her mouth was an olive leaf plucked off: ____ _____ _____ _____ ___

_____ _____ _____ _____

_____ _____ _____.

30. And the Lord smelled a sweet savour; and the Lord said in his heart, ___

_____ _____ _____ _____ _____

_____ _____ _____ _____ _____'s

_____ ;   for the imagination of man's heart is evil _____

_____ _____ . Neither will I again smite any more every

thing living _____ ____ _____ _____.

31. And I will establish my covenant with you; neither shall all flesh be cut off any more by the waters of a flood; neither shall there any more be ___ ____

____ _____ _____ _____ . And God said

_____ ____ ___ _____ ____ _____ _____

_____ _____ _____ _____ _____

____ _____ and every living creature that is with you, for perpetual

generations.

32. I do set _____ _____ _____ _____

and it shall be for a _____ _____ ____ _____

_____ _____ _____ _____ _____.

33. And he drank of the wine _____ _____ _____

and he was uncovered within his tent.

34. And all the days of _____ were nine hundred and fifty years _____ _____ _____ .

35. Now these are the generations of the sons of Noah, _____ , _____ , _____ _____ ; and unto them were sons born after the flood.

36. And the whole earth was of _____ _____ , _____ _____ _____ _____ .

37. Go to, let us go down, and there confound their language that they may _____ _____ _____ _____

38. And Terah lived seventy years, and begat _____ , _____ _____ _____ .

39. And Haran _____ _____ _____ _____ _____ in the land of his nativity, in Ur of the Chaldees.

40. And Abram and Nahor took them wives ; _____ _____ _____ _____ _____ _____ _____ and the name of _____ ' _____ , _____ , the daughter of Haran, the father of Milcah, and the father of Iscah.

41. But Sarai _____ _____ ; she had no children.

42. Now the Lord had said unto Abram, _____ _____ _____ ____ _____ _____ _____ _____ _____ _____ , _____ _____ _____ _____ _____ , unto a land that I will show thee. And I will make thee a great nation, _____ ___ _____ _____ _____ , _____ _____ _____ _____ : _____ _____ _____ _____ .

And I will bless them that bless thee, and curse him that curseth thee: _____

_____ _____ _____ _____ _____

_____ _____ _____ _____ _____.

So Abram departed _____ _____ _____ _____ _____

_____ _____; and Lot went with him; and Abram was seventy
and five years old when he departed out of Haran.

43. Therefore it shall come to pass, when the Egyptians shall see thee, that they
shall say this is his wife _____ _____ _____ _____

_____, but they will save thee alive, say, I pray thee _____ ____

_____ _____; that it may be well with me for thy sake: ____

_____ _____ _____ _____ _____ _____

_____.

44. And Pharaoh commanded his men concerning him: _____ _____

_____ _____ _____ _____ _____ _____,

_____ _____ _____ _____ _____.

45. And Abram was _____ rich in cattle, and in silver, and in gold.

46. And Abram said unto Lot, _____ _____ _____ _____

_____, ___ _____ _____, _____

_____ _____ _____, and between my herdmen and thy herdmen,

_____ _____ _____ _____. Is not the whole land
before thee? Separate thyself, I pray thee, from me: _____ _____

_____ _____ _____ _____ _____, ___

_____ ___ _____ _____ _____ _____; or if thou
depart to the right hand, then I will go to the left.

47. Then Lot chose him _____ _____ _____ _____

_____. And Lot journeyed east; and they separated themselves
the one from the other. Abram dwelled in _____ _____ _____

_____, and Lot dwelled in the cities of the plain, and pitched his tent toward Sodom.

48. For all the land which thou seest, to thee will I give it and to thy seed for ever. And ___ _____ _____ _____ _____ ____ _____ _____ _____ _____ _____ so that if a man can number the dust of the earth, then shall thy seed also be numbered.

49. And they took Lot, Abram's brother's son, _____ _____ ____ _____, and his goods, and departed.

50. And he brought back all the goods, _____ _____ _____ _____ _____ _____ _____, and his goods, and the women also, and the people.

51. And Abram said, behold, ____ _____ _____ _____ _____ _____ _____; and lo, one born in my house is mine heir.

52. And Sarai said unto Abram, behold now, _____ _____ _____ _____ ____ _____ _____; I pray thee, go in unto my maid; it may be that I may obtain children by her. And Abram hearkened to the voice of Sarai.

53. And he went in unto Hagar, _____ _____ _____ and when she saw that she had conceived, _____ _____ _____ _____ ____ _____ _____ _____.

54. And the Angel of the Lord found her _____ ___ _____ ____ _____ in the wilderness, by the fountain in the way to Shur.

55. And the Angel of the Lord said unto her, ___ _____ _____ _____ _____ _____, that it shall not be

_____ for multitude. And the Angel of the Lord said unto her, behold, thy art with child, and shall bare a son, and shall call his name _____ because the Lord hath heard thy affliction.

56. And Hagar bare Abram a son and Abram called his son's name, _____

_____ _____ , _____ .

57. Neither shall thy name any more be called _____, but thy name shall be _____; for a father of many nations have I made thee.

58. This is my covenant, which ye shall keep, between me and you and thy seed after thee; _____ _____ _____ _____

_____ _____ ____ _____ .

And ye shall circumcise the flesh of your foreskin; and it shall be ___

_____ ____ _____ _____

_____ _____ _____ _____ .

59. And God said unto Abraham, _____ _____ _____

thy wife , thou shall not call her name Sarai, _____ _____

_____ _____ _____ _____ .

60. And God said, Sarah thy wife shall _____ _____ ____

_____ _____; _____ _____ _____

_____ _____ _____ _____;

and I will establish my covenant with him for an everlasting covenant, and with his seed after him. And as for _____, I have heard thee; _____, ____ _____ _____

_____, and will make him fruitful, and will multiply him exceedingly;

_____ _____ _____ _____

_____, and I will make him a great nation.

9

61. And all the men of his house, born in the house, and bought with money of the stranger, _____ _____ _____ _____.

62. And Abraham drew near, and said, wilt thou also destroy _____ _____ _____ _____?

63. And the Lord said, if I find ____ _____ _____ _____ _____ _____ _____, then I will spare _____ _____ _____ _____ _____.

64. And it came to pass, when they had brought them forth abroad, that he said, escape for thy life; _____ _____ _____ _____, neither stay thou in all the plain; escape to the mountain, lest _____ _____ _____.

65. Then the Lord rained _____ _____ _____ _____ _____ _____ and _____ from the Lord out of Heaven.

66. But his wife _____ _____ from behind him, and she _____ _____ _____ _____ _____.

67. And the firstborn said unto the younger, _____ _____ ____ _____ and there is not a man in the earth _____ _____ ____ _____ _____ after the manner of all the earth.

68. Thus were both the _____ ____ _____ _____ _____ _____ _____ _____. And the firstborn bare a son, and called his name _____ : the same is the father of the _____ unto this day. And the younger, she bare

a son, and called his name _____-_____; the same is the father of the children of _____ _____ _____ _____.

69. And yet indeed she is my sister; _____ _____ _____ _____

_____ _____ _____, _____ _____

_____ _____ _____ _____ _____

and she became my wife.

70. For Sarah conceived and bare Abraham a son in his old age, at the set time of which God had spoken to him. And Abraham called the name of his son that was born unto him, _____ _____ _____ _____

_____ _____.

71. And Abraham rose up early in the morning, _____ _____

_____, _____ ____ _____ _____ _____,

and gave it unto _____ , putting it on her shoulder, and the child, and sent her away, and she departed and wandered in the wilderness of

_____.

72. Arise, lift up the lad, and hold him in thine hand; _____ ____

_____ _____ _____ ____ _____

_____.

73. And Abraham reproved Abimelech _____ _____

____ _____ ____ _____, which Abimelech's servants had violently taken away.

74. And Abraham took sheep and oxen, and gave them unto Abimelech;

_____ _____ _____ _____ _____ _____

_____.

75. And he said, for these seven ewe lambs, _____ _____

_____ _____ _____ that they may be a _____

_____ _____,   that I have digged this well.

76. And Abraham stretched forth his hand, and took the knife _____

_____ _____ _____.

77. And Abraham lifted up his eyes, and looked, and behold, _____

_____ ___ _____ _____ ____ _____

_____ _____ _____ _____; and

Abraham went and took the ram, and offered him up for a brunt offering ____

_____ _____ ____ _____ _____.

78. That in blessing I will bless thee, and in multiplying I will multiply thy

seed as the _____ ____ _____ _____,

_____ ____ _____ _____ _____ ____

_____ _____ _____ _____; and thy seed shall possess the

gate of his enemies. And in thy seed shall all the nations of the earth be blessed;

_____ _____ _____ _____ _____

_____.

79And Sarah was an hundred and seven and twenty years old; these were the

years of _____ _____ _____ _____.

80. My lord, hearken unto me; _____ _____ _____ _____

_____ _____ _____ _____

_____; What is that betwixt me and thee? Bury therefore, thy dead.

81. And after this, Abraham buried Sarah his wife in the cave of the _____

____ _____ _____ _____; the

same is Hebron in the land of Canaan.

82. And the field, and the cave that is therein, were made sure _____

_____ for a possession of a burying place _____ _____

_____ _____ _____.

83. But thou shalt go unto my country, and to my kindred, and _____ _____ _____ _____ _____ _____ _____.

84. And it came to pass, before he had done speaking, that, behold, _____ _____ _____ , who was born to Bethuel, son of Milcah, the wife of Nahor, Abraham's brother, _____ ___ _____ _____ _____ _____.

85. Behold, Rebekah is before thee, _____ _____, _____ _____, and let her be thy master's son's wife, as the Lord hath spoken.

86. Then again Abraham took a wife, _____ _____ _____ _____ _____. And she bare him _____, and _____, and _____, and _____, and _____, and _____.

87. And Abraham gave all that _____ _____ _____ ____.

88. And these are the days of the years of Abraham's life which he lived, _____ _____ _____ _____ _____ _____.

89. And his sons _____ _____ _____ buried him in the cave of Machpelah, in the field of Ephron the son of Zohar the Hattlte, _____ ____ _____ _____.

90. The field which Abraham purchased of the sons of Heth; _____ _____ _____ _____ _____ _____ _____ _____ _____

91. And the Lord said unto her, _____ _____ _____ _____ _____ _____ and two manner of people shall be separated from thy bowels; and the one people shall be stronger than the other people,

_____ _____ _____ _____ _____

_____ _____. And when her days to be delivered were fulfilled,

behold, there were _____ ____ _____ _____. And

the first _____ _____ _____, _____ _____

_____ ___ _____ _____; and they

call his name _____. And after that came his brother out, and _____

_____ _____ _____ _____ _____'s

_____; and his name was called _____: and Isaac was

threescore years old when she bare them. And the boys grew; and _____

was a cunning hunter, a man of the field; and _____ was a plain

man, dwelling in tents .

92. And Isaac loved Esau, because he did eat of his venison; _____ `_____

_____ _____.

93. And Jacob said swear to me this day; and he sware unto him and _____

_____ _____ _____ _____

_____.

94. Because that Abraham obeyed my voice and kept my charge, _____

_____, _____ _____, _____

_____ _____.

95. And Isaac digged again the wells of water, which they had digged in the day

of Abraham his father; _____ _____ _____

_____ _____ _____ _____ _____

_____ _____ _____; and he

called their names after the names by which his father had called them.

96. And the Lord appeared unto him the same night, and said, _____ _____

_____ _____ _____ _____, _____

_____; _____ _____ _____, _____

_____ _____ _____ _____, _____

_____ _____ _____ and multiply thy seed for my servant Abraham's sake.

97. And they rose up betimes in the morning , and _____

_____ _____ _____; and Isaac sent them away and they _____ _____ _____ _____

_____.

98. And it came to pass, that when Isaac was old, and his eyes were dim, so that he could not see, _____ _____ _____ _____

_____ _____, and said unto him, my son, and he said unto him, behold, here am I.

99. And make me savory meat such as I love, and bring it to me, that I may eat; _____ _____ _____ _____ _____

_____ _____ _____ _____.

100. And Jacob said to Rebekah his mother, behold, Esau my brother _____

_____ _____ _____, _____ ____ ____

____ _____ _____.

101. And she put the skins of the kids of the goat _____ _____

_____, _____ _____ _____ _____

___ _____ _____.

102. And Jacob went near unto Isaac his father; and he felt him, and said ___

_____ ___ _____ _____, _____

_____ _____ _____ _____ ____ _____

_____. and he discerned him not, because his hands were hairy, as his brother Esau's hands ____ ____ _____ _____. And he said, art thou my very son Esau? And he said, _____ _____.

103. And it came to pass, as soon as Isaac had made an end of blessing Jacob, and Jacob was yet scarce gone out from the present of Isaac his father, _____

_____ _____ _____ _____ _____

_____ _____ _____.

104. And he said, thy brother came with subtlety, _____ _____

_____ _____ _____ _____.

105. And he said, is not he rightly named Jacob? For he hath supplanted me these two times: _____ _____ _____ _____

_____, _____ , _____, _____

_____ _____ _____ _____ _____ _____

and he said, hast thou not reserved a blessing for me?

106. And Esau hated Jacob because of the blessing wherewith his father blessed him; and Esau said in his heart,   the days of mouring for my father are at hand; _____ _____ _____ _____

_____ _____ _____.

107.   And he dreamed, and behold a ladder set up on the earth, _____

_____ _____ _____ _____ _____ _____

_____ and behold the angel of God ascending and descending on it.

108. And this stone, which I have set for a pillar, shall be _____ ’____

_____ ; and of all that _____ _____ _____

_____ _____ _____ _____ _____

_____ _____ _____ _____.

109. And he said unto them, is he well? And they said, he is well, and _____,

_____ _____ _____

with the sheep.

110. And Laban had two daughters the name of the _____ _____ _____ and the name of the _____ _____ _____.

111. And Jacob loved Rachel; and said, ____ _____ _____ _____ _____ _____ _____ _____ thy younger daughter.

112. And it came to pass in the evening _____ _____ _____ _____ his daughter and brought her to him _____ _____ _____ _____ _____ _____.

113. And Jacob did so, and fulfilled her week _____ _____ _____ _____ _____ _____ _____ _____ _____ _____.

114. And Leah conceived, and bare a son, and she called his name ____ for she said, surely the Lord hath _____ _____ _____ _____, now therefore my husband will love me.

115. When Leah saw that she had left bearing, _____ _____ _____ _____ _____, _____ _____ _____ _____ _____ _____.

116. And it came to pass, when _____ _____ _____ _____ that Jacob said unto Laban, send me away, that I may go unto _____ _____ _____ and to my country.

117. And the flocks conceived before _____ _____ and brought forth cattle _____, _____, _____ _____.

118. And the man _____ _____ and had much cattle, and maidservants, and menservants and camels, and asses.

119.   And the Lord said unto Jacob, return unto the land of thy fathers, and to thy kindred, _____   ___   _____ _____   _____ _____.

120.   And the angel of God spake unto me in a dream, saying _____; and I said, here am I. and he said, lift up now thine eyes, and see all the _____ _____ _____ _____   _____ _____ _____ _____,   _____ _____ _____; for I have seen all that _____ doeth unto thee. I AM _____   _____ ____ _____-_____ ,   where thou anointest the pillar and where thou _____   ____ _____ _____   _____;   now arise, get thee out from this land, and return unto the land of thy kindred.

121. And Jacob stole away _____   ____   _____ _____ _____ in that he told him not that he fled.

122. And God came to Laban the Syrian in a dream by night and said unto him, _____   _____ _____ _____ _____ _____   _____   _____ _____   _____   _____ _____ ___ _____.

123. And Jacob answered and said to Laban,   _____   ___ _____   _____;   for I said peradventure thou wouldest _____   ____ _____   _____   _____ _____   _____.

124. Thus have I been twenty years in thy house;   ____ _____ _____ _____ _____ _____ _____ _____ _____, and six years for thy cattle and thou hast changed my wages ten times.

125. Now therefore come thou let us _____ _____ _____,
_____ _____ _____; and let it be for a witness between
me and thee.

126. And Mizpah; for he said, the Lord watch between me and thee, _____
_____ _____ _____, _____ _____
_____.

127. This heap be witness, and this pillar be witness, that I _____
_____ _____ _____ _____ _____
_____ _____ and that thou _____ _____ _____
_____ _____ _____ and this pillar unto me _____
_____.

128. And Jacob sent messengers before him _____ _____
_____ unto the land of Seir, the country of Edom.

129. And said, if Esau come to the one company, and smite it, then _____
_____ _____ _____ ___ _____
_____ _____.

130. And Jacob was left alone; and there _____ ___ _____
_____ _____ _____ _____ _____
___ _____ _____.

131. And he said, let me go, for the day breaketh. And he said, _____
_____ _____ _____ _____ _____, _____
_____ _____ _____.

132. And he said, thy name shall be called no more, Jacob, _____
_____ for as a prince hast thou power with God and with men and
hast prevailed.

133. And Jacob called the name of the place Peniel; _____ _____ _____ _____ _____ ___ _____, and my life is preserved.

134. And Esau _____ _____ _____ _____, and embraced him, and fell on his neck, and kissed him _____ _____ _____.

135. But in this will we consent unto you; if ye will be as we be, _____ _____ _____ _____ _____ _____ _____.

136. And it came to pass on the third day, when they were sore, that two of the sons of Jacob, _____ _____ _____, Dinah's brethren, took each man his sword _____ _____ _____ _____ _____ _____, _____ _____ _____ _____ _____.

137. And God said unto Jacob, arise, go up to Beth-el and dwell there; and make there an altar unto God, that appeared unto thee _____ _____ _____ _____ _____ _____ ____ _____ _____ _____.

138. And God said unto him, thy name is Jacob; thy name shall not be called any more Jacob, _____ _____ _____ _____ _____ _____ ; and he called his name Israel. And God said unto him I AM God Almighty; be fruitful and multiply; ____ _____ _____ ____ _____ _____ _____ shall be of thee, and Kings shall come out of thy loins.

139. And God went up from him in the place _____ _____ _____ _____ _____.

140. And it came to pass as her soul was departing (for she   died) that she called his name Ben-oni _____ _____ _____

_____ _____ _____.

141. And Jacob set a pillar upon her grave; _____ _____ _____

_____ _____ _____'s _____ unto

this day.

142. And it came to pass, when Israel dwelt in that land, that Ruben went and lay with Bilhah his _____'s _____; and Israel

heard it. _____ _____ _____ _____ _____

_____ _____.

143. The sons of Leah: _____ , Jacob's firstborn and _____

and _____ and _____ and _____ and

_____.

144. The sons of Rachel; _____ and _____.

145. And the sons of Bilhah Rachel's handmaid _____ and _____.

146. And the sons of Zilpah, Leah's handmaind; _____ and _____;

these are the sons of Jacob, which were born to him in Padan-aram.

147. And the days of Isaac were an hundred and fourscores years. And _____

_____ _____ _____ _____, _____ _____

and was gathered unto his people, being old and full of days; and his sons

_____ and _____ _____ _____.

148. Now these are the generations of Esau, _____ _____ _____.

149. And these are the names of the dukes that came of Esau, according to their families, after their places, by their names: duke _____, duke

_____ duke _____.

150. Now Israel loved Joseph _____ _____ _____ _____

_____, because he was the son of his old age _____ _____

_____ _____ ____ _____ ____ _____

_____.

151. And Joseph dreamed a dream, and he told it his brethren; _____

_____ _____ _____ _____ _____

_____.

152. And they said one to another _____ , _____ _____

_____.

153. And Ruben heard it, and he delivered him out of their hands and said,

_____ _____ _____ _____ _____.

154. And it came to pass, when Joseph was come unto his brethren that they
stripped Joseph out of his coat, _____ _____ _____

_____ _____ that was on him, and they took him, and

cast him into a pit, _____ _____ _____ _____

_____, there was no water in it.

155. Then there passed by Midianites merchantmen; and they drew and lifted up

Joseph out of the pit, _____ _____ _____ _____

_____ _____ _____ _____

_____ _____ _____ ; and they brought Joseph

into _____.

156. And Jacob rent his clothes, and put sackcloth upon his loin, _____

_____ _____ _____ _____ _____

_____ .

157. And Judah acknowledged them, and said, _____ _____ ___

_____ _____ _____ _____:

because that I gave her not to Shelan my son. And he knew her no more.

158. And it came to pass in the time of her travail, that _____,
_____ _____ _____ _____ _____.

159. And Joseph found grace in his sight, and he served him, and _____
_____ _____ _____ _____ _____
_____, and all that he had he put into his hand.

160. And it came to pass after these things, that his master's _____
_____ _____ _____ _____ _____
and she said _____ _____ _____.

161. There is none greater in this house than I; neither hath he kept back anything
from me but thee, because thou art his wife; _____ _____ _____
_____ _____ _____ _____ _____ _____
_____ _____ _____?

162. And she caught him by his garment, saying, _____ _____
_____; and he left his garment in her hand, and fled and got him out.

163. And it came to pass, when his master heard the _____ __ _____
_____ _____, which she spake unto him, saying, after this manner
did thy servant to me ; _____ _____ _____
_____ _____. And Joseph's master took him _____
_____ _____ _____ _____ _____, a
place where the king's prisoners were bond; and he was there in the prison. But the
Lord was with Joseph, and showed him mercy, _____ _____ _____
_____ _____ _____ _____ _____ _____
_____ _____ _____ _____.

164. And they dreamed a dream both of them, _____ _____
_____ _____ _____ _____ _____, each

man according to the interpretation of his dream, _____ _____ _____ _____ _____ of the king of Egypt, which were bound in the prison.

165. And Joseph said unto him, this is the interpretation of it: _____ _____ _____ _____ _____ _____; yet within three days shall Pharaoh lift up thine head, _____ _____ _____ _____ _____ _____ and thou shall deliver Pharaoh's cup into his hand, after the former manner when thou wast his bulter.

166. And Joseph answered and said, this is the interpretation thereof; _____ _____ _____ _____ _____ _____ ; yet within   three days shall Pharaoh lift up thy head from off thee, _____ _____ _____ _____ _____ _____ _____ and the birds shall eat thy flesh from off thee.

167. And he restored the chief butler _____ _____ _____ _____ _____ and he gave the cup into Pharaoh's hand. But he _____ _____ _____ _____ as Joseph had interpreted to them. Yet did not the _____ _____ remember Joseph, _____ _____ _____.

168. And Joseph said unto Pharaoh, the dream of Pharaoh is _____; God hath shown Pharaoh what he is about to do. The _____ _____ _____ are _____ _____; and the _____ _____ _____ are _____ _____: _____ _____ _____ _____.

169. And in the seven plenteous years _____ _____ _____ _____ _____.

170. And the seven years of plenteousness, that was in the land of Egypt,

_____ _____ . And the seven years of dearth began to come

_____ _____ _____ _____ _____

_____; and the dearth was in all lands _____ _____ _____

_____ _____ _____ _____

_____ _____.

171. And all countries came into Egypt to _____ _____

_____ _____ because that the famine was so sore

in all lands.

172. Now when Jacob saw that there was corn in Egypt, Jacob said unto

his sons, _____ _____ _____ _____ _____

_____ _____?

173. And Joseph's _____ _____ went down to buy

corn in Egypt.

174. And Joseph saw his brethren _____ _____ _____ ____,

but made himself strange unto them, and spake roughly unto them, and he

said unto them, whence come ye? And they said, _____ _____

_____ _____ _____ to buy corn.

175. Hereby ye shall be _____; by the life of Pharaoh ye shall

not go forth, _____ _____ _____

_____ _____ _____.

176. And they knew not that Joseph understood them _____ _____

_____ _____ _____ _____ _____

_____.

177. And we said unto him, we are true men; _____ _____ ____

_____.

178. We be twelve brethren, sons of our father; _____ _____ _____,

and the youngest is this day with our father _____ _____ _____

_____ _____.

179. And the men took that _____, and they took _____

_____ in their hand, and _____ and rose up,

and went down to Egypt and stood before Joseph.

180. And when Joseph saw Benjamin with them, he said to the ruler of his house,

_____ _____ _____ _____ _____

_____, _____ _____ _____, _____

_____ _____ _____ _____

_____ _____ _____.

181. And Joseph made haste for his bowels did yearn upon his brother; and he

sought where to weep; _____ _____ _____ _____

_____ _____, _____ _____ _____.

182. And the one went out from me, and I said surely he is torn in pieces,

_____ ____ _____ _____ _____ _____.

183. And Joseph said unto his brethren, _____ _____ ___

_____, I pray you.   And they came near, and he said, ___ _____

_____ _____ _____, _____

_____ _____ _____ _____.

184. And they told him all the words of Joseph, which he had said unto them;

and when he saw the wagons which Joseph had sent to carry him, _____

_____ _____ _____ _____ _____

_____. And Israel said, it is enough; Joseph my son is yet alive; ___

_____ _____ _____ _____ _____ _____

_____ _____.

185. And Jacob rose up from Beer-Sheba _____ _____ _____

_____ _____ _____ _____ _____

_____, and their little ones, and their wives in the wagons which

Pharaoh had sent to carry him.

186. And Joseph made ready his chariot, and went up to meet _____

_____ _____ to Goshen, and presented himself unto him _____

_____ _____ _____ _____ _____, _____

_____ _____ _____ _____ ___ _____

_____. And Israel said unto Joseph, _____ _____ _____

_____, _____ ___ _____ _____

_____ _____, because thou art yet alive.

187. And Joseph brought all the _____ _____ _____

_____ _____ for the Egyptians sold every man his field,

because the famine prevailed over them: ____ _____ _____

_____ _____'s.

188. And Jacob lived in the land of Egypt _____ _____

so the whole age of Jacob was an hundred forty and seven years.

189. But I will lie with my fathers _____ _____ _____

_____ _____ _____ ____ _____ _____ ____

_____ _____ _____ _____.

And he said, I will do as thou hast said.

190.` And his father refused, and said _____ _____ _____ _____

_____, ___ _____ _____; he also shall be great; _____ _____

_____ _____ _____ _____ _____

_____ _____ ____ and his seed shall become ____

_____ _____ _____.

Genesis

191. And Jacob called unto his sons, and said, _____ _____ _____ _____, that I may tell you that which shall befall you in the last days. Gather yourselves together _____ _____, _____ _____ _____ _____; _____ _____ _____ _____ _____ _____.

192. All these are the _____ _____ _____ _____, and this is it that their father spake unto them and blessed them; _____ _____ _____ _____ _____ _____, _____ _____ _____.

193. And he charged them, and said unto them, I am to be gathered unto my people _____ _____ _____ _____ _____ _____ _____ _____ _____ _____ _____ _____ _____ _____ _____ _____ _____ _____. In the cave that is in the _____ _____ _____, which is before Mamre, _____ _____ _____ _____ _____ which _____ bought with the field Ephron the Hittite for a possession _____ _____ _____ _____. There they buried _____ and _____ his wife; there they buried _____ and _____ his wife and there I buried _____. The purchase of the field and of the cave that is therein as _____ _____ _____ _____ _____. And when Jacob had made an end of commanding his sons, he gathered up his feet into the bed and _____ _____ _____ _____, _____ _____ _____ _____ _____.

194. And Joseph fell upon his father' face, and _____ _____ _____ _____ _____ _____. And Joseph commanded his

28

servants the physicians to _____ _____ _____

_____ _____ _____ _____

_____.

195. And Pharaoh said, go up, and bury thy father, _____

_____ _____ _____ _____ _____.

196. And there went up with him both chariots and horsemen: _____

_____ _____ _____ _____ _____

_____.

197. And his sons did unto him according as he commanded them; for his

sons carried him _____ _____ _____ _____

_____ _____ _____ _____, in the

cave of the field of Machpelah, which _____ bought with

the field for a possession of a burying place of Ephron the Hattite, before

_____.

198. So shall we say unto Joseph, forgive, I pray thee now, _____

_____ _____ _____ _____, _____

_____ _____; for they did unto thee evil; and now, we pray

thee, forgive the trespass of the servants of the God of thy father. _____

_____ _____ _____ _____

_____ _____ _____.

199. But as for you ye thought evil against me; _____ _____

_____ _____ _____ _____, to bring to pass, as

it is this day.

200. And Joseph said unto his brethren, I die; and God will surely visit you, and

bring you out of this land unto the   land which he sware _____ _____

_____ _____, _____ _____ _____.

201.   And Joseph took an oath of _____ _____ ___

_____,   saying, God will surely visit you, _____ _____

_____ _____ _____ _____ _____

_____ _____. So Joseph died, being an hundred and ten

years old; and they embalmed him, and he was put in a coffin in _____.

The End   GENESIS

EXODUS

1. Now these are the names of the _____ _____ _____,

which came into Egypt; every man and his household came with _____.

2. And Joseph died, and all his brethren, _____ _____ _____

_____.

3. And he said unto his people, behold, the people of the children of Israel

_____ _____ _____ _____ _____ _____.

4. And the Egyptians made _____ _____ ____ _____

to serve with rigour.

5. And Pharaoh charged all his people, saying, _____ _____

_____ ___ _____ _____ _____ _____

_____ _____ _____, and every daughter ye shall

save alive.

6. And when she had opened it _____ _____ _____ _____

and behold, _____ _____ _____ and she had compassion

on him, and said this is one of _____ _____ _____

_____.

7. And the child grew, and she brought him unto _____'s

_____, _____ _____ _____ _____

_____. And she called his name _____; and she said, _____

___ _____ _____ _____ _____ _____

_____.

8. And he looked this way and that way and when he saw that there was no man,

_____ _____ _____ _____ _____

_____ _____ _____ _____ _____.

9. Now when Pharaoh heard this thing, _____ _____

_____ _____ _____. But Moses fled _____

_____ _____ _____ _____ and dwelt in the

land of Midian: and sat down by a well.

10. And Moses was content to dwell with the man: _____ _____

_____ _____ _____ _____ _____.

And she bare him a son, and he called his name _____ for

he said, I have been a stranger in _____ _____

_____.

11. And God heard their groaning and God remembered his Covenant with

_____, _____ _____, _____ _____

_____.

12. Now Moses kept the flock of Jethro his father-in-law, the priest of Midian:

_____ ____ _____ _____ _____ _____ ____

_____ _____ _____ _____, and

came to the mountain of God, even to Horeb.

13. And Moses said, I will now turn aside, and see this great sight, _____

_____ _____ ____ _____ _____.

14. And he said, draw not nigh hither: _____ _____ _____ _____

_____ _____ _____ _____, _____ _____

_____ _____ _____ _____ ____

_____ _____.

15. Come now therefore, and I will send thee unto Pharaoh, that thou mayest

_____ _____ _____ _____

_____ ____ _____ _____ ____

_____.

16. And God said unto Moses I AM THAT I AM. And he said, thus shalt thou say unto the children of Israel ____ _____ _____ _____ ____

_____ _____.

17. Go and gather the elders of Israel together, and say unto them, the Lord God of Abraham, of Isaac, and of Jacob appeared unto me, saying, ____

____ _____ _____ _____, _____ _____

____ _____ ____ _____ ____ _____ ____

_____. And I have said, ___ _____ _____

_____ _____ _____ _____ _____ _____

_____ _____ unto the land of Canaanites, and the Hittites and the Amorites, and the Perizzites, and the Hivites, and the Jebusites, _____

___ _____ _____ _____ _____

_____ _____.

18. And I will stretch out my hand, and smite Egypt _____ _____

_____ _____ which I will do in the midst thereof; and

_____ _____ ___ _____ _____ _____

_____.

19. And the Lord said unto him, what is that in thine hand? And he said, ____

_____.

20. And Moses said unto the Lord, O my Lord, ____ _____ _____

_____ , neither heretofore, nor since thou hast spoken unto thy

servant: _____ ___ _____ _____ ____ _____,

_____ _____ ____ _____ _____.

21. Now therefore go, and I will be with thy _____, _____

_____ _____ _____ _____ _____

_____.

22. And the anger of the Lord was kindled against Moses, and he said, ____

_____ _____ _____ _____ _____

_____? ____ _____ _____ ____

_____ _____ _____. And also, behold, he cometh

forth to meet thee: and when he seeth thee _____ _____ _____

_____ _____ _____ _____.

23. And he shall be thy _____ _____ _____

_____: and he shall be, even he shall be to thee instead of a mouth,

and _____ _____ _____ _____ _____

_____ _____ _____.

24. And Moses took his wife and his son, and set them upon an ass _____

_____ _____ _____ _____ _____

_____: and Moses took _____ _____ _____

_____ _____ _____ _____.

25. And Aaron spoke all the words _____ _____ _____

_____ _____ _____ _____, and did the signs

in the sight of the people.

26. And afterward Moses and Aaron went in, and told Pharaoh, thus saith the

Lord God of Israel, _____ _____ _____ _____, that they

may hold a feast unto me in the wilderness. And Pharaoh said, who is the Lord,

_____ ____ _____ _____ _____ _____ _____

_____ _____ _____ _____? I know not the Lord, _____

_____ _____ _____ _____ _____.

27. For since I came to Pharaoh to speak in thy name, he hath done evil to this people, _____ _____ _____ _____

_____ _____ _____ _____.

28. And God spake unto Moses and said unto him I AM _____ _____. And I appeared unto Abraham, unto Isaac, and unto Jacob, by the name of _____ _____ but by my name _____ _ _____ ___ _____ _____ ____ _____. and I have also established a _____ with them to give them the land of Canaan, the land of their pilgrimage, _____ _____ _____ _____.

29. And the Lord said unto Moses, see, I have made thee a god to Pharaoh: _____ _____ _____ _____ _____ ____ _____ _____.

30. And Moses and Aaron went in unto Pharaoh, and they did so as the Lord had commanded: and Aaron cast down his rod before Pharaoh, and before his servants, _____ _____ _____ ___ _____.

31. For they cast down every man his rod, and they became serpents but _____'s _____ _____ ____ _____ _____.

32. And Moses and Aaron did so, as the Lord commanded; and he lifted up the rod, and smote the waters that were in the river, ____ _____ _____ _____ _____, and in the sight of his servants, _____ _____ _____ _____ _____ _____ _____ _____ _____ _____.

33. And the Lord spake unto Moses , say unto Aaron, _____

_____ _____ _____ _____ _____

_____over the streams, over the rivers and over the ponds and _____

_____ _____ _____ ____ _____ _____

_____ ____ _____.

34. And the Lord said unto Moses, say unto Aaron, stretch out thy rod and smite the dust of the land, _____ _____ _____ _____

_____ _____ _____ _____ _____ ____

_____.

35. And the Lord did so; and _____ _____ ____ _____

_____ ____ _____ into the house of Pharaoh, and into his servants' houses and into all the land of Egypt; _____ _____

_____ _____ _____ _____ ____ _____

_____ _____ _____.

36. And the Lord did that thing on the morrow, and all the cattle of Egypt died;

_____ _____ _____ _____ ____ _____

_____ ____ _____ _____

_____ _____.

37. And it shall become small dust in all the land of Egypt, and shall _____

___ _____ _____ _____ _____

_____ _____ _____, and upon beast, throughout all the land of Egypt.

38. Behold, tomorrow about this time ___ _____ _____

____ ____ _____ ___ _____ _____

_____ such as hath not been in Egypt since the foundation thereof even until now.

39.   And the Lord said unto Moses stretch out thine hand over the land of Egypt _____ _____ _____ that they may come up upon the land of Egypt, and _____ _____ _____ ____ _____

_____ _____ _____ _____ _____ _____

_____ _____ .

40. And the Lord said unto Moses, stretch out thine hand _____

_____ , _____ _____ _____ ____

_____ over the land of Egypt, even darkness which may be felt.

41. And Moses and Aaron did all these wonders before Pharaoh: and the Lord hardened Pharaoh's heart ____ _____ ____ _____

_____ _____ _____ _____ ____ _____

____ _____ _____ _____ _____ .

42. And they shall take of the blood, and strike it on _____ _____

_____ _____ _____ _____ _____ _____

_____ _____ _____ _____ _____ , wherein they shall eat it.

43. And the blood shall be to you for ____ _____ _____

_____ _____ _____ _____ _____ : ___

_____ ___ _____ _____ _____ , ___

_____ _____ _____ _____ and the plague shall not be upon you to destroy you, when I smite the land of Egypt.

44.   And ye shall observe this thing for a ordinance to thee and to thy sons _____ _____ .

45. That ye shall say, ____ _____ _____ _____

____ _____ _____ 's _____ , who passed over the houses of the children of Israel in Egypt, when he smote the Egyptians, and delivered our houses. _____ _____ _____ _____

_____ _____ _____ _____.

46. And it came to pass, that at midnight the Lord smote all the firstborn in the land of Egypt, from the _____ ____ _____ that sat on his throne unto the firstborn of the captive that was in the dungeon; and _____ _____ _____ _____ _____.

47. And Pharaoh rose up in the night, he, and all his servants, and all the Egyptians; and there was a great cry in Egypt; _____ _____ _____ _____ ___ _____ _____ _____ _____ _____ _____ _____.

48. And he called for Moses and Aaron by night, and said _____ ____,

_____ _____ _____ _____ _____ _____ _____ _____ both ye and the children of Israel; and go, _____ _____ _____ , as ye have said.

49. And the children of Israel did according to the word of _____; and they borrowed of the Egyptians jewels of silver and jewels of gold, and raiment. And the Lord gave the people _____ ____ _____ _____ ____ _____ _____, so that they lent unto them _____ _____ _____ _____ _____. And they spoiled the Egyptians.

50. And it came to pass the selfsame day, that the Lord did bring the _____ _____ _____ out of the land of Egypt by their armies.

51. And the Lord spake unto Moses, saying, sanctify unto me all the _____ _____ , whatsoever openeth the womb among _____ _____ _____ _____, both of man and of beast: _____ _____ _____.

52. And it shall be for a _____ upon thine hand, and for frontlets between thine eyes; _____ _____ _____ _____ _____ the Lord brought us forth _____ _____ _____.

53. And Moses took _____ _____ _____ _____ _____ _____: for he had straitly sworn the children of Israel saying God will surely visit you; _____ _____ _____ _____ _____ _____ _____ _____ _____ _____ _____.

54. And the Lord went before them by day _____ ____ _____ _____ _____, to lead them the way; and by night ____ ___ _____ _____ _____, to give them light to go by day and night.

55. And I will harden Pharaoh's heart, _____ _____ _____ _____ _____ _____; and I will be honored upon Pharaoh, and upon all his host; that the Egyptians _____ _____ that ___ _____ the Lord. And they did so.

56. And Moses said unto the people, _____ _____ _____, _____ _____, _____ _____ _____ _____ _____ _____ _____, which he will show to you today; for the Egyptians whom ye have seen today, ye shall see them again _____ _____ _____ _____. The Lord shall fight for you, _____ ____ _____ _____ _____ _____.

57. And Moses stretched out his hand over the sea; and the Lord caused the sea to go back by a strong _____ _____ all that night, and _____ _____ _____ _____ _____ and the waters were divided. And _____ _____ ____ _____ went into the midst of the sea upon the _____ _____ and the

38

waters were a wall unto them on their _____ _____ _____

_____ _____ _____.

58. And the waters returned, and covered the chariots, and the horseman, and all the host of Pharaoh that came into the sea after them: _____

_____ _____ _____ _____ _____ _____

_____ _____.

59. Then sang Moses and the children of Israel this song unto the Lord, and spake, saying, _____ _____ _____ _____ _____

_____, _____ _____ _____ _____

_____; _____ _____ _____ _____

_____ _____ _____ _____ _____

_____ _____.

60. And Miriam the prophetess, _____ _____ _____

_____ took a timbrel in her hand; and all the women went out after her _____ _____ _____ _____

_____.

61. And the people murmured against Moses, saying, _____ _____

_____ _____? And he cried unto the Lord and the _____

_____ _____ ___ _____, which when he had cast into the waters, _____ _____ _____ _____ _____;

there he made for them a statute and an ordinance, and there he proved them.

62. And said, if thou wilt diligently hearken to the voice of the Lord thy God

_____ _____ _____ _____ _____ _____

_____ _____ _____ _____, and wilt give ear to his commandments and keep all his statutes, I will put none of these _____

_____ _____, which I have brought upon the Egyptians; _____

_____ _____ _____ _____ _____ _____

_____.

63. Then said the Lord unto Moses , behold, ___ _____ _____

_____   _____   _____   _____   _____;

and the people shall go out and gather a certain rate every day, _____

_____ _____ _____ _____, whether they will walk

in my law or no.

64. And Moses said, this shall be when the Lord shall give you in the evening

flesh to eat, and in the morning bread to the full; for that the Lord heareth your

murmurings which ye murmur against him; and what are we? _____

_____   _____   _____   _____   _____,

_____   _____   _____   _____.

65. Six days ye shall gather it; but on the seventh day, which is the _____,

_____   _____   _____   _____   _____   _____.

66. Behold, I will stand before thee there upon the rock in Horeb; and thou

shalt smite the rock, _____ _____ _____ _____

_____   _____   _____   _____ that the people may drink.   And

Moses did so in the sight of the elders of Israel.

67. And it came to pass on the morrow, that Moses sat to judge the people; and

the people _____ _____ _____ _____ _____

_____   _____   _____   _____.

68. And Moses said unto his father-in-law, _____ _____

_____   _____   _____   _____   _____   _____

_____   _____. When they have a matter, they come unto me; _____

____   _____   _____   _____   _____

_____, and I do make them know the statutes of God, and

his laws.

69. And Moses chose able men out of all Israel, and make them heads over the

people, rulers of thousands, rulers of hundreds, rulers of fifties and rulers of tens.

And they judged the people at all seasons; _____ _____ _____

_____ _____ _____ _____ but every

small matter they judged themselves.

70. And Moses went up unto God, and the _____ _____

_____ _____ out of the mountain, saying, , thus shall thou say to the

house of Jacob, and tell the children of Israel; ye have seen what I did unto

the Egyptians _____ _____ _____ _____ _____ _____

_____ _____, _____ _____ _____

_____ _____. Now therefore, if ye will obey my voice

indeed, and keep my _____, then ye shall be a _____

_____ unto me above all people; for all the earth is mine. And

ye shall be unto me a kingdom of priests, and an holy nation. _____

_____ _____ _____ _____ _____

_____ _____ _____ _____ _____

_____ _____.

71. And all the people saw the _____, and the _____,

and the noise of the _____, and the mountain _____;

and when the people saw it, they removed, and stood afar off.

72. Read/list/underline the TEN COMMANDMENTS.

73. And the Lord said unto Moses, thus thou shalt say unto the children of Israel

_____ _____ _____ _____ ___ _____ _____

_____ _____ _____ _____.

74. And he that smiteth his father or his mother, _____ _____

_____ _____ ____ _____.

75. If the theft be certainly found in his hand alive, whether it be ox or ass or

sheep _____ _____ _____ _____.

76. But if thou shalt indeed _____ _____ _____, _____ _____ _____ _____ ____ _____: then I will be an enemy unto thine enemies and an adversary unto thine adversaries.

77. And he said unto Moses, come up unto the Lord, _____ _____ _____, _____, _____ _____ _____ seventy of the elders of Israel, and worship ye afar off.

78. And Moses came and told the people all the words of the Lord, and all the judgments; and all the people answered with one voice, and said _____ ____ _____ _____ _____ _____ _____ _____ _____ _____ _____. And Moses wrote all the words of the Lord, and rose up early in the morning, and built an altar under the hill, and _____ _____, according to _____ _____ _____ _____ _____.

79. And Moses took the blood, and _____ _____ _____ _____ _____, _____ _____, _____, _____ _____ _____ _____ _____, which the Lord hath made with you concerning all these words.

80. And Moses went into the midst of the cloud, and got him up into the mount _____ _____ _____ ____ _____ _____ _____ _____ _____ _____ _____.

81. Speak unto the children of Israel, that they _____ _____ ____ _____; of every man that giveth it willingly with his heart ye shall take my offering

82. Oil for light, _____ _____ _____ ___ and for sweet incense.

83. Thou shalt also make a _____ _____ _____

_____; two cubits shall be the length thereof, and a cubit the breadth

thereof _____ ___ _____ _____ ___ _____ _____

_____ _____.

84. Moreover thou shalt make the tabernacle with ten curtains of fine twined

linen, and blue, and purple, and scarlet; _____ _____

____ _____ _____ _____ _____

_____ _____.

85. And thou shall make a covering for the tent _____ _____ _____

_____ _____ and a covering above _____ _____,

_____.

86. And thou shalt make _____ _____ of shittim wood, five cubits long,

and five cubits broad; and the altar shall be foursquare: and the height thereof

_____ _____ _____ _____.

87. Hollow with boards shalt thou make it: _____ _____ _____

_____ _____ _____ _____ _____,

so shall they make it.

88. And thou shall make holy garments _____ _____ _____

_____ _____ _____ _____ _____

_____.

89. And thou shalt take two onyx stones, and grave on them _____

_____ _____ _____ _____ _____ _____:

six of their names on one stone and other six names of the rest on the stone,

_____ _____ _____ _____.

90. And thou shall put them upon Aaron thy brother, and his sons with him;

_____ _____ _____ _____, _____

_____ _____, _____ _____

_____ that they may minister unto me in the _____'s

_____.

91. Then shall thou take the _____ _____, _____

_____ _____ _____ _____ _____, and anoint

him.

92. And they shall eat those things wherewith _____ _____

_____ _____, _____ _____ _____

_____ _____ _____: but a stranger shall not eat thereof,

because they are holy.

93. And they shall know that _____ _____ _____ _____

_____ _____, that brought them forth out of the land of Egypt,

that I may dwell among them; _____ _____ _____ _____

_____ _____.

94. And the rich shall not give more, _____ _____ _____

_____ _____ _____ _____ _____ _____

___ _____, when they give an offering unto the Lord to make an

_____ for your souls.

95. I have filled him _____ _____ _____ ___ _____,

in wisdom, and in understanding, and in knowledge, and in all manner of

workmanship.

96. Speak thou also unto the children of Israel, saying, verily Sabbath ye shall

keep _____ ____ _____ ____ _____ _____

_____ _____ _____ throughout your generation that ye may know

that I am the Lord that doth sanctify you.

97. And all the people brake off the golden earrings which were in their ears,

_____   _____   _____   _____   _____.

98. And the Lord said unto Moses _____ , _____ _____ _____ ,
for thy people, which thou broughtest out of the land of Egypt, _____
_____   _____.

99. And the Lord said unto Moses, I have seen this people, and, behold, _____

_____   ____   _____   _____.

100. And the Lord _____ of the evil which he thought to ____

_____   _____   _____.

101. And it came to pass, as soon as he came nigh unto the camp, that _____

_____   _____   _____ ,   _____   _____   _____ , and
Moses anger waxed hot, and he cast the tables out of his hands, and _____

_____   _____   _____   _____.

102. Then Moses stood in the gate of the camp, and said, _____ ____

_____   _____   _____'s   _____? Let him come unto me.
And _____   _____   _____   _____   _____ gathered
themselves together unto him.

103. And the Lord said unto Moses, whosoever hath sinned against me, _____

_____   ____   _____   _____   _____   _____

_____.

104. And Moses took _____   _____ and pitched it without
the camp, afar off from the camp, and called it _____ _____ ____
_____   _____ . And it came to pass, that every one
which sought the Lord went out unto the tabernacle of the congregation, which
was without the camp.

105. And the Lord said unto Moses, I will do this thing also that thou hast spoken: _____ _____ _____ _____ _____

____ _____ _____, _____ _____ ____ _____

_____ ____ _____.

106. And the Lord said unto Moses, hew thee two tables of stone like unto the first; and I will write upon these tables the words that were in the first tables, _____ _____ _____.

107. For thou shall worship no other god: for the Lord, whose name is jealous, _____ ___ _____ _____.

108. But the _____ of an ass thou shall redeem with a lamb; and ____ _____ _____ _____ _____, then shalt thou break his neck. All the _____ of any sons thou shall redeem.

_____ _____ _____ _____ _____

_____ _____.

109. And the Lord said unto Moses, write thou these words; for after the tenor of these words ___ _____ _____ ___ _____

_____ _____ _____ _____ _____. And he was there with the Lord _____ _____ _____ _____

_____; he did neither eat bread, nor drink water. And he wrote

_____ _____ _____ _____ _____ ____ _____

_____, _____ _____ _____. And it came to pass, when Moses came down from _____ _____ with the two tables of testimony in Moses' hand, when he came down from the mount, that Moses wist not that _____ _____ _____ _____

_____ _____ _____ ____ _____

_____ _____. And when Aaron and all the children of Israel saw Moses, behold, _____ _____ ____ _____ _____

_____. And they were afraid to come nigh him.

110. And till Moses had done speaking with them, _____ _____ ___
_____ _____ _____ _____.

111. And Moses gathered all the congregation of the children of Israel together,
and said unto them, these are words which the Lord hath _____,
_____ _____ _____ _____ _____.

112. And Moses said unto the children of Israel, see, the Lord hath called by
name _____ _____ _____ _____ _____,
_____ _____ _____ _____, _____ _____ _____
_____ _____. and he hath filled _____ _____
_____ _____ _____ _____, in wisdom, in understanding,
and in knowledge, and in all manner of workmanship.

113. And he hath put _____ _____ _____ _____ _____
_____ _____, both he and Aholiab, the son of Ahisamach, of
_____ _____ _____ _____.

114. And they spake unto Moses saying, _____ _____
_____ _____ _____ _____ _____ for
the service of the work, which the Lord commanded to make.

115. And the five pillars of it with their hooks; and he overlaid their chapters and
their fillets with gold: _____ _____ _____ _____
_____ _____ _____.

116. And he made his seven lamps, and his snuffers, and his snuffdishes _____
_____ _____.

117. And he made _____ _____ _____ _____
and the pure incense of sweet spices, according to the work of the apothecary.

118. This is the sum of the tabernacle even of the tabernacle of testimony as it
was counted, according to the commandment of Moses, _____ _____

_____ ____ _____ _____ by the hand
of _____, _____ ____ _____ _____
_____.

119. And Bezaleet the son of _____, the son of _____, _____
_____ _____ _____ _____, made all that the Lord
commanded Moses.

120. And of the blue, and purple, and scarlet, they made cloth of service, to do
service in the holy place, _____ _____ _____ _____
_____ _____ _____, as the Lord commanded
_____.

121. Thus was all the work of the tabernacle of the tent of the congregation
finished: and the children of Israel did according to all that the Lord commanded
_____ ____ _____ _____.

122. And Moses did look upon all the work, _____ _____,
_____ _____ _____ ____ ____ _____ _____
_____ _____, even so had they done it; _____
_____ _____ _____.

123. And Moses and Aaron and his sons _____ _____
_____ _____ _____ _____ _____;
when they _____ _____ the tent of the congregation, and when
they _____ _____ unto the altar, _____ _____
as the Lord commanded Moses. And he reared up the court round about the
tabernacle and the altar and set up the _____ ____ _____
_____ _____. So Moses finished the work. Then a cloud
covered the tent of the congregation _____ _____ _____

____ _____ _____ _____ _____
_____.

124. For the cloud of the Lord was upon the tabernacle _____ _____

_____ _____ _____ _____ _____ _____ _____,

in the sight of all the house of Israel, throughout all their journeys.

The End EXODUS

LEVITICUS

1. If his offering be a burnt sacrifice of the herd, _____ _____ _____

___ _____ _____ _____:he shall offer

it of his own voluntary will at the door of the tabernacle of the congregation

_____ _____ _____. And he shall put his hand upon the

head of the burnt offering; and it shall be _____ _____

_____ _____ _____ _____ _____

_____.

2. And when any will offer meat offering unto the Lord, his offering _____

___ _____ _____ _____ _____; _____ _____

_____ _____ _____ ____, and put frankincense

thereon.

3. As for the oblation of the _____, _____ _____

_____ _____ _____ _____ _____:

but they shall not be burnt on the altar for a sweet savour.

4. And if his oblation be a sacrifice of _____ _____, if he

offer it of the herd; whether it be a male or female, he shall offer it _____

__ _____ _____ _____ _____.

5. If the priest that is anointed do sin _____ _____

_____ _____ _____ _____ _____; then let

him bring for his sin, which he hath sinned, a young bullock without blemish unto the Lord _____ ___ _____ _____ .

6.   And if a soul sin, and commit any of these things which are forbidden to be done by the commandments of the Lord though he wist it not, yet is he guilty,

_____ _____ _____ _____ _____ .

7.   And the priest shall make an _____ _____

_____ before the Lord: and it shall be forgiven him for any thing of all that he hath done ____ _____ _____ .

8.   And the priest shall burn the fat upon the altar: but the breast shall be _____'s _____ _____ _____ .

9. And Moses took the anointing oil, _____ _____

_____ _____ and all that was therein, _____

_____ _____ .

10. And he poured of the anointing oil upon _____'s _____,

_____ _____ _____ to sanctify him.

11. Aaron therefore went unto the altar, and slew the calf of the sin offering,

_____ _____ _____ _____ .

12. And Aaron lifted up his hand _____ _____

_____, _____ _____ _____, and came down from offering of the _____ offering, and the _____ offering, and _____ _____ .

13. And Nadab and Abihu, the _____ ____ _____, took either of his censer, and put fire therein, and put incense thereon, and offered _____ _____ before the Lord, _____ _____

_____ _____ _____ . And there went out fire from

the Lord and _____ _____, _____ _____

_____ _____ _____ _____.

14. And Moses spake unto Aaron, and unto Eleazar and unto Ithamar, _____

_____ _____ _____ _____, take the meat offering that

remained of the offering of the Lord made by fire, and eat it without leaven beside

the altar : _____ _____ _____ _____ _____.

15. These shall ye eat of all that are in the waters: whatsoever hath _____

_____ _____ in the waters, in the sea, and in the rivers, _____

_____ _____ _____.

16. For I AM the Lord that bringeth you up out of the land of Egypt, to be

your God: ye shall therefore be holy, _____ ' _____ _____

_____.

17. Speak unto the children of Israel, saying, _____ ___ _____

_____ _____ _____, _____ _____

_____ _____ _____: _____ she shall be unclean seven days;

according to the days of the separation for her infirmity shall she be unclean.

And in the eighth day _____ _____ _____ _____ _____

_____ _____ _____ _____.

18. And the priest shall look on the plague in the skin of the flesh: _____

_____ _____ _____ ____ _____ _____

_____ _____ _____, and the plague in sight be

deeper than the skin of his flesh, _____ _____ _____ _____

_____ _____: and the priest shall look on him, and

pronounce him _____.

19. Then the priest shall consider: and , behold, _____ _____ _____

_____ _____ _____ _____ _____ he

shall pronounce him clean that hath the plague; it is all turned white: _____

_____ _____.

20. This is the law of the plague of leprosy in a garment of woollen or linen, either in the warp, or woof, or any thing of skin, _____ _____ ___ _____ ____ _____ _____ ____ _____.

21. And he that is to be cleansed shall wash his clothes, and shave off all his hair, and wash himself in water, that he may be clean: and after that he shall _____ _____ _____ _____ and shall tarry abroad out of his tent _____ _____.

22. And the Lord spake unto _____ and unto _____, saying, when ye be come into _____ _____ _____ _____ which I give to you for a possession, and I put the _____ ____ _____ in a house of the land of your possession: and he that owneth the house shall _____ _____ _____ _____ _____, saying, it seemeth to me there is as it were _____ _____ _____ _____ _____.

23. To teach when it is _____, and when it is _____: this is the law of leprosy.

24. And the vessel of earth, that he toucheth which hath the issue, shall be broken: _____ _____ _____ _____ _____ _____ ___ _____ _____ _____.

25. And the priest shall offer them, the one for a sin offering, and the other for a burnt offering, and the priest shall make _____ _____ for him before the Lord for his issue.

26. But if she be cleansed of her issue, then she shall _____ ____

_____ _____ _____.

27. And he shall make an atonement for the holy place, because of the

_____ ____ _____ _____ __

_____, and because of their _____

____ _____ _____ _____: and so shall he do for the

tabernacle of the congregation, that remained among them in the midst of their

uncleanness.

28. For on that day shall the priest _____ ____ _____

_____ _____, to cleanse you, that ye may be clean _____ _____

_____ _____ before the Lord. It shall be a _____

____ _____ _____ _____, and ye shall afflict your souls,

by a statue for ever.

29. And this shall be an _____ _____ _____

_____, to make an atonement for the _____ _____

_____ for all their sins _____ ___ _____. And

he did as the Lord commanded Moses.

30. And the priest shall sprinkle the blood _____ _____ _____

____ _____ _____ at the door of the _____

____ _____ _____, and burn the fat for a sweet savour

unto the Lord.

31. But if he wash them not, nor bathe his flesh: _____ _____

_____ _____ _____ _____.

32. Ye shall therefore keep my statutes, and my judgments: _____

_____ ___ _____ _____, he shall live in them: I AM the

Lord.

33. None of you shall approach to any _____ ____ _____ _____ _____ _____ _____ to uncover their nakedness: I AM the Lord.

34. Moreover thou shall not lie carnally with thy neighbor's wife, _____ _____ _____ _____ _____.

35. And the Lord spake unto Moses, saying, speak unto all _____ _____ of the children of Israel, and say unto them ye shall be _____: for I the Lord your God AM _____.

36. And if ye offer a sacrifice of peace offering unto the Lord, ye shall offer it _____ _____ _____ _____.

37. Ye shall not steal, neither deal falsely, _____ _____ _____ ____ _____.

38. If a man also lie with mankind, _____ ____ _____ _____ ___ _____, both of them have committed an abomination; they shall surely be put to death; their blood shall be upon them.

39. And ye shall be _____ unto me: for I the Lord am holy, and have severed you from other people, _____ ____ _____ _____ _____.

40. But he shall not defile himself, _____ ____ _____ _____ _____ _____ _____, to profane himself.

41. And Moses told it unto Aaron, and to his sons, and _____ _____ _____ _____ ____ _____.

42. That which dieth of itself, or is torn with beasts, _____ _____

_____ _____ _____ _____ _____ _____

_____: I AM the Lord.

43. That brought you out of _____ _____ _____ _____,
to be your God: I AM the Lord.

44. Speak unto the children of Israel, and say unto them, concerning _____

_____ _____ _____ _____ which ye shall proclaim to

be _____ _____, even these are my feasts.

45. And the Lord spake unto Moses, saying, speak unto the children of Israel,

and say unto them, _____ _____ _____ _____ _____ _____

_____ _____ ___ _____ _____ _____,

and shall reap the harvest thereof, then ye shall bring a _____ _____

_____ _____ ___ _____ _____

_____ _____ _____.

46. And ye shall do no work in that same day; _____ _____ _____ ____

_____ _____ _____, to make an atonement for you

before the _____ _____ _____.

47. And Moses declared unto _____ _____ _____
_____ the feast of the Lord.

48. Command the children of Israel, that they bring unto thee _____

_____ _____ _____ for the light, to cause the lamps to

burn _____.

49. Speak unto the children of Israel, and say unto them, when ye come into the

land which I give you, then shall the land _____ _____ _____

_____ _____ _____. Six years thou shalt sow thy field,

and _____ _____ thou shalt prune thy vineyard, and gather in the fruit thereof; but in the _____ _____ shall be a _____ ____ _____ unto the land, a _____ for the Lord; thou shalt neither sow thy field, nor prune thy vineyard.

50. Then shall thou cause the trumpet of the jubilee to sound on _____ _____ _____ ____ _____ _____ _____, in the day of atonement shall ye make the trumpet sound throughout all your land.

51. Then I will command my _____ _____ _____ ____ _____ _____ _____, and it shall bring forth fruit for three years.

52. For unto me the children of Israel are servants; _____ _____ _____ _____ whom I brought forth out of the land of Egypt: I AM the Lord your God.

53. Ye shall keep my Sabbath _____ _____ _____ _____: I AM the Lord.

54. If ye walk in my statutes, and keep my commandments, _____ _____ _____; then I will give you rain in _____ _____, and the land shall yield her _____ and the trees of the field shall yield their fruit.

55. And five of you shall _____ _____ _____ and an hundred of you shall put _____ _____ _____ _____: and your enemies shall fall before you by the sword. For I will have _____ _____ _____, and make you fruitful and multiply you, _____ _____ _____ _____ _____ _____.

56

56.　 I AM the Lord your God, which brought you forth out of the land of Egypt, that ye should not be their bondmen; and _____ _____ _____ _____ _____ ____ _____ _____, and made you go upright.

57.　 Then will I also walk contrary unto you , and will punish you yet _____ _____ _____ _____ _____.

58.　 If they shall confess their iniquity,   and the iniquity of their fathers , with their trespass which they trespassed against me, and that also _____ _____ _____ _____ _____ ____; and that I also have walked contrary unto them, and have brought them into the land of their enemies; ____ _____ _____ _____ _____ ____ _____, and they then accept of the punishment of their iniquity.   Then will I _____ __ ____ _____ _____ _____, _____ _____ _____ _____ _____ _____, _____ _____ ____ _____ _____ _____ _____ ___ _____ and I will remember the land.

59.　 And the Lord spake unto Moses, saying, speak unto the children of Israel, and say unto them, _____ ____ _____ _____ _____ ____ _____ _____, the persons shall be for the Lord by thy estimation.

60. Only the firstling of the beasts, _____ _____ _____ _____ _____'s _____, no man shall sanctify it; whether it be ox, or sheep; _____ _____ _____ _____'s.

61. And all the tithe of the land, whether of the seed of the land, or of the fruit of the tree, ____ _____ _____'s: ____ ____ _____ _____ _____ _____.

62. And concerning the tithe of the herd, or of the flock, even of whatsoever passeth under the rod, _____ _____ _____ _____ _____ _____ _____ _____.

63. These are the commandments , which the Lord commanded _____ for the children of Israel in Mount Sinai.

The End LEVITICUS

NUMBERS

1. And the Lord spake unto Moses ____ _____ _____ _____ _____ in the tabernacle of the congregation, on the first day of the second month, ____ _____ _____ _____ after they were come out of the land of Egypt, saying, take ye the sum of all the congregation of the children of Israel, after their families, by the house of their fathers, _____ _____ _____ _____ _____ _____, every male by their polls: from twenty years old and upward, all that are able to go forth to war in Israel. _____ _____ _____ _____ _____ _____ _____ _____ _____.

And with you there shall be a man ____ _____ _____; every one head of the house of his fathers.

2. Even all they were numbered were _____ _____ _____ _____ _____ _____ _____ _____ _____ _____ _____.

But the Levites after the tribe of their fathers were not numbered among them.

3. But thou shall _____ _____ _____ _____ _____ _____ _____, and over all the vessels thereof, and over all things that belong to it; they shall

bear the tabernacle, and all vessels thereof; and they shall minister unto it, and shall encamp round about the tabernacle.

4. Every man of the children of Israel shall _____ _____ _____ _____ _____, with the ensign of their father's house; for off about the tabernacle of the congregation _____ _____ _____.

5. Then the tribe of Benjamin and the captain of the sons of Benjamin shall be

_____ _____ _____ _____ _____.

6. And Nadab and Abihu _____ _____ _____ _____, _____ _____ _____ _____ _____ before the Lord, in the wilderness of Sinai, and they had not children; and Eleazar and Ithamar ministered in the priest's office in the sight of _____ _____ _____.

7. And they shall keep his charge, _____ _____ _____ of the whole congregation before the tabernacle of the congregation, to do _____ _____ ____ _____ _____.

8. In the number of all the males, from a month old and upward were eight thousand and six hundred, _____ _____ _____ _____ _____ _____.

9. And Moses numbered, as the Lord commanded him, _____ _____ _____ _____ the children of Israel.

10. And Moses took _____ _____ _____ of them that were over and above them that were redeemed by the _____.

11. This shall be the service of the _____ _____ _____ in the tabernacle of the congregation, about _____ _____ _____ _____.

12. And Moses and Aaron and the _____ _____ _____
_____ numbered the sons of the Kohathites after their families,
and after the house of their fathers.

13. According to the commandment of the Lord _____ _____
_____ _____ _____ _____ _____ _____,
every one according to his service, and according to his burden; thus were they
numbered of him _____ _____ _____ _____
_____.

14. Command the children of Israel, that they put out of the camp _____
_____, _____ _____ _____ _____ _____
_____ _____, and whosoever is defiled by the dead.

15. And the priest shall write these curses in a book , _____ _____
_____ _____ _____ _____ with the bitter
water.

16. Then shall the man be guiltless from iniquity, and this woman _____
_____ _____ _____.

17. Speak unto the children of Israel, and say unto them, when either man or
woman shall separate themselves _____ _____ _____ _____ _____
_____ _____, to separate themselves unto the Lord. He shall
separate himself from _____ _____ _____ _____
and shall drink no vinegar of wine, or vinegar of strong drink, neither shall
he drink any liquor of grapes, _____ _____ _____
_____ _____ _____.

18. All the days of the vow of his separation there _____ _____
_____ _____ _____ _____ _____;
until the days be fulfilled, in the which he separateth himself unto the Lord, he

shall be holy,   and shall let the locks of the hair _____ _____ _____

_____.

19. All the days that he separateth himself unto the Lord, he shall come at _____

_____   _____.

20. All the days of his separation he is _____ _____ _____

_____.

21. And this is the law of the Nazarite _____ _____ _____

_____ _____ _____ _____ _____;

he shall be brought unto the door of the _____ _____

_____ _____.

22. But unto the sons of Kohath _____ _____ _____:
because the service of the sanctuary belonging unto them was that they should

_____ _____ _____ _____.

23. On the fourth day Elizur the son of Shedeur, _____ _____

_____ _____ _____ _____, _____

_____.

24. On the nineth day Abidan the son of Gideoni, _____ _____

_____ _____ _____ _____,

_____.

25. On the twelfth day Ahira the son of Eran, Prince of the children of

_____, _____.

26. Speak unto Aaron, and say unto him, when thou lightest the lamps _____

_____ _____ _____ _____ _____

_____ _____ the candlestick.

27. And the Levites were purified, and they washed their clothes; and Aaron offered them as an offering before the Lord; _____ _____ _____ _____ _____ _____ _____ _____ _____ _____.

28. And from the age of _____ _____ they shall cease waiting upon the service thereof _____ _____ _____ _____ _____.

29. Let the children of Israel also keep _____ _____ _____ _____ _____ _____.

30. And Moses said unto them, _____ _____, and I will hear what the Lord will command _____ _____.

31. So it was always ; the cloud covered it by day, and the appearance _____ _____ _____ _____.

32. And when they shall blow with them, _____ _____ _____ _____ _____ _____ _____ _____ at the door of the tabernacle of the congregation.

33. And the children of Israel took their journeys out of _____ _____ _____ _____ and the cloud rested in the wilderness of Paran.

34. And the tabernacle was taken down and the sons of Gershon and the sons of Merari set forward, _____ _____ _____.

35. And it came to pass when the art set forward that Moses said, rise up, Lord, and let thine enemies be scattered; _____ _____ _____ _____ _____ _____ _____ _____ _____.

36. And when the people _____, it displeased the Lord; and the Lord heard it, _____ _____ _____ _____ _____; and the fire of the Lord burnt among them, _____ _____ _____ _____ _____ in the uttermost parts of the camp.

37. I am not able to bear all this people alone, _____ _____ _____ _____ _____ _____ _____.

38. And the Lord said unto Moses, gather unto me _____ _____ _____ _____ _____ _____ _____, whom thou knowest to be the elders of the people, and officers over them; and bring them unto the tabernacle of the congregation that they may stand there with thee.

39. And Joshua the son of Nun, the servant of Moses , one of his young men, answered and said, _____ _____ _____, _____ _____.

40. And while the flesh was _____ _____ _____ _____, ere it was chewed, the wrath of the Lord was kindled against the people, and the Lord smote the people with a very great plague. And he called the name of that place Kibroth-hattaavah; because there they _____ _____ _____ _____ _____.

41. And Miriam and Aaron spake against Moses _____ _____ _____ _____ _____ _____ _____ _____; for he had married an Ethiopian woman.

42. And the Lord came down in the pillar of the cloud, and stood in the door of the tabernacle, _____ _____ _____ _____ _____: and they both came forth.

43. And the anger of the Lord _____ _____ _____
_____, and he departed.

44. And the cloud departed from off the tabernacle; and behold, _____
_____ _____, _____ _____ _____;
and Aaron looked upon Miriam, and , behold, _____ _____
_____.

45. And Miriam was shut out from the camp _____ _____; and
the people journeyed not til _____ _____ _____
_____ _____ .

46. And Moses by the commandment of the Lord sent them from the wilderness
of Paran; _____ _____ _____ _____ _____
_____ _____ _____ _____ _____ .

47. And Moses sent them to spy out _____ _____ _____
_____, and said unto them, get you up this way southward, and
go up into the mountain.

48. And they returned from searching of the land _____ _____
_____ .

49. And they told him, and said, we came unto the land whither thou sentest us,
and _____ _____ _____ _____ _____
_____ _____; and this is the fruit of it.

50. And they brought up an evil report of the land which they had searched
unto the children of Israel, saying, the land through which we have go to search
it, _____ _____ _____ _____ _____ _____
_____ _____ _____; and all the people
that we saw in it _____ _____ _____ _____ _____
and we saw the _____; and Anak, which come of the gaints; and

we were in our own sight _____ _____ and we were in their sight.

51. I the Lord have said, I will surely do it unto all this evil congregation, _____ _____ _____ _____ _____ ___; in this wilderness they shall be consumed, and there they shall die. And the men, which Moses sent to search the land, who returned, _____ _____ _____ _____ _____ _____ _____ _____ _____, by bring up a slander upon the land. Even those men that did bring up the _____ _____ _____ _____ _____, _____ ____ _____ _____ before the Lord. But _____ the son of Nun, and _____ the son of Jephunneh, which were of the men that went to search the land _____ _____.

52. According to the number that ye shall prepare, so shall ye do to _____ _____ _____ _____ _____ _____.

53. One law and one manner shall be for you and for the _____ _____ _____ _____ _____.

54. And the priest shall make an atonement for the _____ _____ _____ _____, when he sinneth by ignorance before the Lord, to make an atonement for him; _____ _____ _____ _____ _____ _____.

55. And they that found him gathering sticks brought him unto _____ _____ _____, _____ _____ _____ _____ _____.

56. That ye may remember, and do all my commandments, _____ _____ _____ _____ _____ _____.

Numbers

57. And Korah gathered all the congregation against them unto the door of the tabernacle of the congregation; _____ _____ _____

_____ _____ _____ _____ _____ _____

_____ _____. And the Lord spake unto Moses and unto Aaron, saying, separate yourselves from among this congregation, _____

_____ _____ _____ _____ _____ ___

_____.

58. And the earth opened her mouth, and _____ _____

_____, and their houses, and all the men that appertained unto Korah, and all their goods.

59. And thou shalt write _____'s _____ _____

_____ _____ _____ _____; for _____ _____

shall be for the head of the house of their fathers.

60. And it shall come to pass, that the man's rod, whom I shall choose, _____ _____; and I will make to cease from me the murmurings of the children of Israel, whereby they murmur against you.

61. And Moses laid up the _____ before the Lord in the tabernacle of witness. And it came to pass, that on the morrow Moses went into the tabernacle of witness; and , behold, _____ _____ ___ _____

_____ _____ _____ ____ _____ _____

_____, and brought forth buds, and bloomed blossoms, and

_____ _____.

62. And the Lord said unto Moses, bring Aaron's rod again before the testimony, ____ ____ _____ ____ ___ _____ _____

_____ _____, and thou shall quite take away their murmurings from me, that they die not.

An Invitation To Know Him

63. And I, behold, I have taken your brethren the Levites from among the children of Israel: to you they are given as a gift for the Lord, ____ ____

_____ _____ ___ _____ _____ ____

_____ _____ .

64. All the best of the oil, and all the best of the wine, and of the wheat, _____

_____ _____ _____ _____ _____

_____ _____ _____ _____ _____ ,

them have I given thee.

65. And , behold, I have given the children of Levi all the tenth in Israel for an inheritance, _____ _____ _____ _____

_____ _____ , even the service of the tabernacle of the congregation.

66. Thus speak unto the Levites, and say unto them, when ye take of the children of Israel _____ _____ which I have given you _____

_____ _____ _____ _____ , then ye shall offer up an heave offering of it for the Lord, _____ ___ _____

_____ _____ _____ _____ .

67. And Eleazar the priest shall take of her blood with his finger, and sprinkle of her blood directly before the tabernacle of the congregation _____

_____ .

68. And a man that is clean shall gather up the ashes of the heifer, and lay them up without the camp in a _____ _____ , and it shall be kept for the congregation of the children of Israel for a water of separation: _____

_____ ____ _____ _____ _____ .

69. Then came the children of Israel, even the whole congregation, into the desert of Zin in the first month: and the people abode in Kadesh; and _____

67

_____ _____ , _____ _____ _____
_____ .

70. And Moses lifted up his hand, and with his rod he _____ ___
_____ _____ and the water came out abundantly and the
congregation drank and their beasts also.

71. And the Lord spake unto Moses and Aaron, because ye believed me not, to
sanctify me in the eyes of the children of Israel, _____ ____
_____ _____ bring this congregation into the land which I have
given them.

72. Aaron shall be gathered unto his people; _____ ____ _____
_____ _____ _____ _____ _____ which
I have given unto the children of Israel, because ye rebelled against my word
at the water of Meribah.

73. And Moses stripped Aaron of his garments, and put them upon Eleazar his
son , _____ _____ _____ _____ _____
_____ _____ ___ _____ _____ : and Moses and Eleazar
came down from the mount.

74. And the Lord sent fiery serpents among the people, and they bit the people;
and much _____ ___ _____ _____ .

75. And the Lord said unto Moses, make thee a fiery serpent and _____
___ _____ ___ _____ ; and it shall come to pass, that every
one that is bitten, when he looketh upon it, _____ _____ . And
Moses made a serpent of brass and put it upon a pole, that if a serpent had bitten
any, when he beheld the serpent of brass, _____ _____ .

76. The Israel sang this song, _____ _____ , __ _____ ,
_____ ____ _____ ____ .

77. And the Lord said unto Moses, fear him not; _____ ____ _____
_____ _____ _____ _____ _____, and all
his people, and his land, and thou shalt do to him as thou didst unto Sihon King
of the Amorites, which dwelt at Heshbon.

78. Behold, there is a people come out of Egypt, which covereth the face of
the earth: _____ _____ _____ _____ _____;
preadventure I shall be able to overcome them and _____ _____
_____.

79. And Balaam rose up in the morning, and saddled his ass, and went with the
princes of Moab. And God's anger was _____ _____
____ _____: and the angel of the Lord stood in the way for an adversary
against him. Now he was riding upon his ass, and his two servants were with
him. And the ass saw the _____ ____ _____ _____
_____ _____ _____ _____ and his sword drawn
in his hand; and the ass turned aside out of the way, and went into the field;
_____ _____ _____ _____ _____, _____
_____ _____ _____ _____.

80. And the ass saw me, and turned from me these three times unless she had
turned from me, _____ _____ _____ ___ _____
_____ _____, _____ _____ _____ _____.

81. How shall I curse, whom God hath _____ _____? Or
how shall I defy, whom the Lord hath _____ _____?

82. Behold, I have received commandment to bless: and he hath blessed: and
___ _____ _____ ____.

83. But Balaam answered and said unto Balak, told not I thee, saying, all that
the Lord speaketh, _____ ___ _____ _____.

84. And Balaam lifted up his eyes, and he saw Israel abiding in his tents according to their tribes; _____ _____ _____ ____

_____ _____ _____ _____.

85. And he took up his parable, and said, Balaam the son of Beor hath said, and the man whose eyes are open hath said; he hath said which heard the words of God, and knew _____ _____ ____ _____

_____ _____, which saw the vision of the Almighty, _____

_____ ___ _____, but having his eyes open.

86. And he went after the man of Israel into the tent, and thrust both of them through, _____ _____ ____ _____, _____ _____

_____ _____ _____ _____. So the plague was stayed from the children of Israel. And those that died in the plague were

_____ _____ _____ _____.

87. And it came to pass after the plague, that the Lord spake unto Moses and unto Eleazar the son of Aaron the priest saying, take the _____ ____

_____ _____ _____ of the children of Israel, from twenty years old and upward, throughout their father's house, all that are able to go to war in Israel.

88. And the Lord spake unto Moses, saying, unto these the land shall be divided _____ ____ _____ according to the number of names.

89. But among these there _____ _____ ____ _____ whom Moses and Aaron the priest _____, when they numbered the children of Israel in the wilderness of Sinai.

90. And the Lord spake unto Moses, saying, the daughters of _____

_____ _____: Thou shall surely give them a possession of an inheritance among their father's brethren; and thou shalt cause the inheritance _____ _____ _____ _____ _____

_____ _____.

91. And the Lord said unto _____, get thee up into this mount Abarim, _____ _____ _____ _____ which I have given unto the children of Israel. And when thou hast seen it, _____ _____ _____ _____ _____ _____ _____ _____, as Aaron thy brother was gathered.

92. And Moses spake unto the Lord, saying, let the Lord, _____ _____ _____ _____ _____ _____ _____, set a man over the congregation.

93. And Moses did as the Lord commanded him: and he took _____, _____ _____ _____ _____ _____ _____ _____ and before all the congregation: and he _____ _____ _____ _____ _____ and gave him a charge as the Lord commanded by the hand of Moses.

94. And the Lord spake unto Moses, saying, command the children of Israel, and say unto them, _____ _____, _____ _____ _____ _____ _____ _____ _____ _____ _____, for a sweet savour unto me, shall ye observe to offer unto me in their due season.

95. And a several tenth deal of flour mingled with oil for a meat offering unto one lamb; for a burnt offering of a sweet savour, ___ _____ _____ _____ _____ _____ _____ _____.

96. And in the seventh month, on the first day of the month, _____ _____ _____ _____ _____ _____ _____; ye shall do no servile work; it is a day of blowing the trumpets unto you.

97. These things ye shall do unto the Lord in your set feasts, _____

_____ _____ _____ _____ _____

_____, for your burnt offerings, and for your meat offerings, and

for your drink offerings, and for your peace offerings.

98. If a man vow a vow unto the Lord, or swear an oath to bind his soul with a

bond; _____ _____ _____ _____ _____

_____, he shall do according to all that _____ _____

_____ _____ _____.

99. And they warred against the Midianites, as the Lord commanded Moses;

_____ _____ _____ _____ _____ _____.

100. Everything that may abide in the fire, ye shall make it go through the fire,

and it shall be clean _____ _____ _____ _____

_____ _____ _____ _____ _____

_____; and all that abideth not the fire ye shall make go

through the water.

101. And divide the prey into two parts; between them that took the war upon

them, who went out to battle, and between all the _____.

102. And Moses and Eleazar the priest took the gold of the captains of thousands

and of hundrens, and brought it into the tabernacle of the congregation, _____

___ _____ for the children of Israel before the Lord.

103. And the Lord's anger was kindled the same time, and he sware saying,

surely none of the men that came up out of Egypt, from twenty years old and

upward, shall see the land which I sware _____ _____,

_____ _____ _____ _____ _____;

because they have not wholly followed me. Save _____ the son of

Jephunneh the Kenezite, _____ _____ the son of Nun; for

they have _____ _____ _____ _____.

72

And the Lord's anger was kindled against Israel, And he made them wander in the wilderness _____ _____, until all the generation, that had done evil in the sight of the Lord, _____ _____.

104. And Moses said unto them, if the children of _____ and the children of _____ will pass with you _____ _____, every man armed to battle, before the Lord, and the land shall be subdued before you; then ye shall give them the land of Gilead for a possession.

105. But if they will not pass over with you armed, they shall have possessions among you in the _____ ____ _____.

106. And Moses wrote their goings out according to their journeys by the commandment of the Lord; and these _____ _____ _____ _____ ____ _____ _____ _____.

107. Then ye shall drive out all the inhabitants of the land from before you, and destroy all their pictures, and destroy all their molten images, and quite pluck down _____ _____ _____ _____.

108. But if ye will not drive out the inhabitants of the land from before you; then it shall come to pass, that those which ye let remain of them shall be _____ ____ _____ _____, _____ _____ ____ _____ _____, and shall vex you in the land wherein ye dwell.

109. And the Lord spake unto Moses, saying, command the children of Israel, and say unto them, when you come into _____ _____ _____ _____; (this is the land that shall fall unto you for an inheritance, even the land of Canaan with the coast thereof).

110. These are the names of the men which shall divide the land unto you; _____ _____ _____, _____ _____ _____ _____ ____ _____.

73

111. These are they whom the Lord commanded to divide the inheritance unto the children of Israel in the land of _____.

112. And the suburbs of the cities, which ye shall give unto the _____, shall reach from the wall of the city and outward a thousand cubit round about.

113. Ye shall give three cities on this side of Jordan, and three cities shall ye give in the land of canaan, _____ _____ _____ _____ _____ _____.

114. Defile not therefore the land which ye shall inhabit, wherein I dwell: _____ _____ _____ _____ _____ _____ the children of Israel.

115. This is the thing which the Lord doth command concerning the _ _____ ____ _____ , saying, let them marry to whom they think best; only to the family of the tribe of their father _____ _____ _____.

116.   These are the commandments and the judgments, which the Lord commanded by the hand of _____ unto the children of Israel in the plains of Moah by Jordan near _____.

THE END NUMBERS

DEUTERONOMY

1. And it came to pass in the fortieth year, in the eleventh month, on the first day of the month, _____ _____ _____ _____ _____ _____ ____ _____, according unto all that the Lord had given him in commandment unto them.

2. Behold, I have set the land before you: go in and possess the land which the Lord _____   _____   _____   _____, Abraham, Isaac and Jacob to give unto them and to their seed after them.

3. Yet in this thing ye did not _____   _____   _____ _____   _____, who went in the way before you, to search you out a place to pitch your tent _____   _____   ____   _____ to show you by what way ye should go, and _____   ____   _____ _____   _____.

4. And the Lord said unto me, say unto them, _____   _____   _____, neither fight; _____   ____   _____   _____   _____   _____ _____ lest ye be smitten before your enemies.

5. And the Amorites, which dwelt in that mountain,   came out against you , _____   _____   _____,   _____   _____   _____ and destroyed you in Seir, even unto Hormah.

6. Meddle not with them; for I will not give you of their land, no not so much as a foot breadth; _____   ____   _____   _____ _____   _____   _____   _____   _____ ____   _____.

7. For the Lord thy God hath _____   _____ in all the works of thy hand; he knoweth thy walking through this great wilderness;   these forty years the Lord thy God hath been with thee; _____   _____ _____   _____.

8. For indeed the hand of the Lord was against them to destroy them from among the host, _____   _____   _____   _____.

9. And the Lord our God delivered him before us _____   _____   _____ _____   _____   _____   _____, and all his people.

Deuteronomy

10. So the Lord our God delivered into our hands Og also, the king of Bashan, and all his people; and we smote him until _____ _____ _____ _____ _____ _____.

11. But charge _____, and encourage him, and strengthen him; for he shall go over before this people, _____ ____ _____ _____ _____ ____ _____ _____ _____ which thou shalt see.

12. Ye shall not add unto the word which I command you, _____ _____ ____ _____ _____ _____ ____, that ye may keep the commandments of the Lord your God which I command you.

13. Keep therefore and do them; for this is _____ _____ _____ _____ _____ in the sight of the nation, which shall hear all these statutes, and say, surely this great nation is a wise and understanding people.

14. And he declared unto you his _____ which he commanded you to perform, even ten commandments and _____ _____ _____ _____ _____ _____ _____ _____.

15. But I must die in this land, ____ _____ _____ _____ _____ but ye shall go over, and possess that good land.

16. But if from thence thou shalt seek the Lord thy God, thou shalt find him, ____ _____ _____ _____ _____ _____ _____ _____ _____ _____ _____ _____ _____ _____.

17. (for the Lord thy God is a merciful God) _____ _____ _____ _____ _____, neither destroy thee, _____ _____ _____ _____ ____ _____ _____ which he sware unto them.

18. Unto thee it was shown, that thou mightest know that the Lord he is God; _____ ____ _____ _____ _____ _____.

19. And because he loved thy fathers, therefore he chose their seed after them, and brought thee out in his sight with _____ _____ out of Egypt.

20. Know therefore, this day, and consider it in thine heart, that the Lord he is God _____ _____ _____, and upon earth beneath. There is none other.

21. And Moses called all Israel, and said unto them, _____, _____ _____, the statutes and judgments which I speak in your ears this day, that ye may learn them, and keep and do them. The Lord our God made a _____ with us in Horeb. The Lord _____ _____ _____ _____ _____ _____ _____, but with us. Even us, who are all of us here alive this day.

22. These words the Lord spake unto all your assembly in the mount out of the midst of the fire, of the cloud, and of the thick darkness, with a _____ _____ and he added no more. And he wrote them in _____ _____ ____ _____, and delivered them unto me.

23. Ye shall walk in all the ways which the Lord your God hath commanded you, that ye may live, and that it may be well with you, _____ _____ ____ _____ _____ _____ _____ in the land which ye shall possess.

24. Hear therefore, O Israel, and observe to do it, that it may be well with thee

_____ _____ ____ _____ _____ _____,

as the Lord God of thy fathers hath promised thee, _____ _____ ____

_____ _____ _____ _____ _____

_____,   Hear O Israel; the   Lord our God ____ _____

_____. And thou shall love the Lord thy God with all thine heart, and

with all thy soul, and with all thy might. And these words, which I command

thee this day shall be in thine heart .

25. And thou shall do that which is right and good ___ _____

_____ ____ _____ _____: that it may be well with

thee, and that thou mayest go in and possess the good land which the Lord sware

unto my fathers.

26. For thou are an holy people unto the Lord thy God: the Lord thy God hath

chosen thee to be a _____ _____ _____

_____, above all people that are upon the face of the earth.

27. Know therefore that the Lord thy God, he is God, the faithful God which

keepeth _____ _____ _____ with them that love

him and keep his commandments _____ ____ _____

_____.

28. And the Lord will take away from thee _____ _____,

and will put none of the evil diseases of Egypt, which thou knowest, _____

_____; but will lay them upon all them that _____ _____.

29. And thou shalt _____ all the way which the Lord thy

God led thee these _____ _____ in the wilderness,

____ _____ _____, _____ ____ _____

_____, to know what was in thine heart whether thou wouldest keep

his commandments or no.

30. Therefore thou shalt keep the commandments of the Lord thy God, _____ _____ ___ _____ _____, _____ ____ _____ _____.

31. But thou shalt remember the Lord thy God; _____ ____ ____ ____ _____ _____ _____ _____ _____ _____ _____, that he may establish his _____ which he sware unto thy fathers, ____ ____ ____ _____ _____.

32. And the Lord was very angry with _____ _____ _____ _____ _____: and I prayed for Aaron also the same time. And I took your sin, _____ _____ _____ ____ _____ _____ and burnt it, and ground it very small, _____ _____ _____ _____ _____ _____ _____ _____ and I cast the _____ thereof into the brook that descended out of the mount.

33. And he wrote on the tables, according to the first writing, _____ _____ _____, which the Lord spake unto you in the mount _____ ____ _____ _____ ____ _____ _____ in the day of the assembly: and the Lord gave them unto me.

34. Circumcise therefore the foreskin of your heart, _____ _____ __ _____ _____.

35. Love ye therefore the stranger : _____ _____ _____ _____ _____ _____ _____ ____ _____.

36. And what he did unto Dathan and Abiram, the sons of Eliab, the son of _____: _____ _____ _____ _____ _____ _____ _____ _____ _____ _____, and their households, and their tents, and all the substance that was in their possession, ____ _____ _____ _____ _____ _____.

79

37. Therefore shall ye lay up these my _____ in your heart and in your soul, and bind them for a sign upon your hand, that _____ ____ _____ ____ _____ _____ _____ _____.

38. And ye shall observe to all the _____ _____ _____ _____ which I set before you this day.

39. And thither ye shall bring your _____ _____, and your _____, and your _____, and _____ _____ of your hand and your _____ and your _____ _____ _____ and the _____ of your herds and of your flocks.

40. Observe and hear all these words which I commend thee, that it may go well with thee, _____ _____ _____ _____ _____ _____ _____ _____, when thou doest that which is good and right in the sight of the Lord thy God.

41. What thing soever I command you, observe to do it: _____ _____ _____ _____ _____, _____ _____ _____ _____.

42. Thou shalt not hearken unto the words of _____ _____, ____ _____ _____ _____ _____: for the Lord your God proveth you, to know whether ye love the Lord your God with all your heart and with all your soul.

43. And every beast that parteth the hoof, and cleaveth the cleft into two claws, and cheweth the cud among the beast, _____ _____ _____ _____.

44. And every creeping thing that flieth is _____ unto you: _____

_____ _____ _____ _____.

45. At the end of _____ _____ _____ thou shalt

make a _____.

46. For the Lord thy God blesseth thee, as he promised thee: and _____

_____ _____ _____ _____ _____,

_____ _____ _____ _____ _____;

and thou shalt reign over many nations, _____ _____ _____

_____ _____ _____ _____.

47. And when thou sendest him out free from thee, _____ _____

_____ _____ _____ _____ _____ _____

48. Observe the month of Abib, and keep the Passover unto the Lord thy God:
for in the month of Abib the Lord thy God brought thee forth _____ _____

_____ _____ _____.

49. Seven week shalt thou number unto thee; begin to number the seven weeks
from such time as thou beginnest to _____ _____ _____ _____

_____ _____.

50. Thou shalt observe the feast of tabernacle _____ _____,
after that thou hast gathered in thy corn and thy wine.

51. That which is _____ _____, shalt thou follow, that
thou mayest live, and inherit the land which the Lord thy God giveth thee.

52.   At the mouth of two witnesses, or three witnesses, shall he that is worthy
of death be put to death; but at the mouth of one witness _____ _____

_____ _____ _____ _____ _____.

53. And it shall be, when he _____ _____ _____ ____ _____ _____, that he shall write him a copy of this law in a book out of that which is before the priest the Levites.

54. The Lord thy God will raise up unto thee ____ _____ _____ _____ _____ _____ _____, of thy brethren, like unto me, unto him ye shall hearken.

55. When a prophet speaketh in the name of the Lord, if the thing _____ _____, _____ _____ ____ _____, that is the thing which the Lord hath _____ _____, but the prophet hath spoken it presumptuously; thou shalt not be afraid of him.

56. And those which remain shall hear, and fear, and shall henceforth commit ____ _____ _____ _____ _____ _____ _____.

57. For the Lord thy God is he that goeth with you, to fight for you against your enemies, _____ _____ _____.

58. If one be found slain in the land which the Lord thy God giveth thee to possess it, lying in the field, and it be not known _____ _____ _____ _____.

59. And they shall answer and say, our hands have not shed this blood, _____ _____ _____ _____ _____ _____.

60. But he shall acknowledge the son of the hated for _____ _____ _____, _____ _____ _____ _____ _____ ____ _____ _____ ____ _____:

for he is the beginning of his strength; the right of the firstborn is his.

61. The woman shall not wear that which pertained unto a man, neither shall a man put on a woman's garment: _____ _____ _____ _____ _____
_____ _____ _____ _____ _____
_____ _____.

62. A man shall not take his father's wife, _____ _____
_____ _____'s _____.

63. That which is gone out of thy lips thou shalt keep and perform; even a freewill offering, according as thou hast _____ unto the Lord thy God, _____ _____ _____ _____
_____ _____ _____.

64. Remember what the Lord thy God did unto _____ by the way, after that ye were come forth out of Egypt.

65. The fathers shall not be put to death for the children, neither shall the children be put to death for the fathers: _____ _____ _____
_____ _____ _____ _____ _____ _____
_____ _____.

66. If there be a controversy between men, and they come unto judgement, that the judges may judge them; then they _____ _____
_____ _____, _____ _____ _____
_____.

67. And his name shall be called Israel, the house of him that _____
_____ _____ _____.

68. That thou shalt take of the first of all the fruit of the earth, which thou shalt bring of thy land that the Lord thy God giveth thee, _____ _____
_____ _____ _____ _____ _____, and shalt go unto the place which the Lord thy God shall cooose to place his name there.

69. And now, behold, I have brought the _____ of the land, which thou, ___ _____, _____ _____ _____. And thou shalt set it before the Lord thy God and worship before the Lord thy God.

70. When thou hast made an end of tithing all the tithes of thine increase the third year, _____ ___ _____ _____ ___ _____, and hast given it unto the _____, _____ _____, _____ _____ _____ _____ _____ that they may eat within thy gates, and be filled.

71. Look down from thy holy habitation, from heaven, _____ _____ _____ _____ _____, and the land which thou hast given us, as thou swaredt unto our fathers, ___ _____ _____ _____ _____ _____ _____ _____.

72. And Moses and the priests the Levites spake unto all Israel, saying, _____ _____, _____ _____ ____ _____; this day thou art become the people of the Lord thy God. Thou shall therefore _____ _____ _____ _____ ____ _____ _____ _____ _____, and do his commandments and his statutes, which I command thee this day.

73. Cursed be he that lieth with his _____'s _____; because he uncovered his father's _____. And all the people shall say; _____.

74. And it shall come to pass, if thou shalt hearken diligently unto the _____ of the Lord thy God to observe and to do all his commandments which I command thee this day, that the Lord thy God _____ _____ _____ ____ _____ _____ _____ _____ ____ _____ _____ _____: and all these blessing shall come on thee, _____ _____ _____ if thou shalt hearken unto the _____ of the Lord thy God.

84

75. Blessed shalt thou be when _____ _____ _____ and blessed shall thou be when _____ _____ _____.

76. The Lord shall cause thine enemies that rise up against thee to be smitten before thy face; they shall come out _____ _____ _____ _____, _____ _____ _____ _____ _____ _____.

77. The Lord shall make thee the head, _____ _____ _____ _____; and thou shalt be _____ _____ and thou shalt _____ ____ _____ if that thou hearken unto the commandments of the Lord thy God, which I command thee this day, to observe and _____ _____ _____.

78. But it shall come to pass, if thou wilt _____ hearken unto the _____ of the Lord thy God, to observe ____ ____ _____ his commandments and his statutes which I command thee this day; that all these _____ _____ _____ _____ _____, _____ _____ _____.

79. And ye shall be left few in number, whereas ye were _____ _____ _____ _____ _____ _____ _____ because thou wouldest not obey the _____ of the Lord thy God.

80. These are the words of the covenant, which the Lord commanded Moses to make with the _____ _____ _____ in the land of Moab, beside _____ _____ _____ _____ _____ _____ ____ _____.

81. Keep therefore the words of this covenant, and do them, _____ ____ _____ _____ ____ _____ _____ ____ _____.

82. The secret things belongs unto the Lord our God; _____ _____ _____ _____ _____ _____ _____ _____ _____ and our children for ever, that we may do all the words of this law.

83.   I call heaven and earth to record this day against you, that I have set before you life and death, blessing and curse: _____ _____ _____, _____ _____ _____ _____ _____ _____ _____ _____.

84. That thou mayest love the Lord thy God, and that thou mayest _____ _____ _____, and that thou mayest cleave unto him: _____ ____ ____ _____ _____, _____ _____ _____ ____ _____ _____; that thou mayest dwell in the land which the Lord sware unto thy fathers, ____ _____, ____ _____ _____ ____ _____, to give them.

85. And Moses went and spake these words unto all Israel. And he said unto them, I am an hundred and twenty years old this day; ___ _____ ____ _____ ____ _____ _____ _____ ____: also the Lord hath said unto me, _____ _____ _____ _____ _____ _____ _____.

86. And Moses called unto Joshua, and said unto him in sight of all Israel, ____ _____ _____ ____ _____ _____: for thou must go with this people unto the land which the Lord hath sworn unto their fathers to give them; _____ _____ _____ _____ _____ ____ _____ _____.

87. And the Lord said unto Moses, behold, thy days approach that thou _____ _____: call _____ and present yourselves in the tabernacle of the congregation, _____ ___ _____ _____

_____ ___ _____. And Moses and Joshua went, and presented themselves in the tabernacle of the congregation.

88. That Moses commanded the Levites, _____ _____

_____ _____ _____ _____ _____ of the Lord saying, take this book of the law and _____ _____ _____ _____

_____ _____ _____ _____ _____ _____ _____ of the Lord your God, that it may be there for a witness against thee.

89. Because I will   publish the name of the Lord;   ascribe ye _____

_____ _____ _____.

90. Remember the days of old, consider the years of many generation; ask thy father, _____ _____ _____ _____ _____; thy elders and _____ _____ _____ _____.

91. And Moses came and spake all the words of this song in the ears of the people, he, and Hoshea _____ _____ _____ _____.

92. And the Lord spake unto Moses that selfsame day, saying, get thee up into this mountain Abarim, _____ _____ _____, which is in the land of Moah, _____ ____ _____ _____ _____; and behold the land of Canaan which I give unto the children of Israel for a possession. And _____ in the mount whither thou goest up, and be gathered unto thy people as Aaron thy brother _____ _____

_____ _____ and was gathered unto his people.   Because ye trespassed against me among the children of Israel at the waters of Meribah-Kadesh, _____ _____ _____ _____ _____; because ye sanctified me not in the midst of the children of Israel. Yet thou shalt see the land before thee, _____ _____ _____ _____

_____ _____ _____ _____ _____ which I give the children of Israel.

93. And this is the blessing, wherewith Moses the man of God blessed the children of Israel _____ _____ _____.

94. And of Joseph he said, blessed of the Lord be his land for the _____ _____ ____ _____, for the dew, and for the deep that coucheth beneath.

95. And the Lord said unto him, this is the land which I sware unto Abraham, unto Isaac and unto Jacob, saying, I will give it unto thy seed; I have caused thee to see it with thine eyes, _____ _____ _____ _____ ____ _____ _____. _____ _____ _____ _____ ____ _____ _____ _____ _____ ____ _____ _____ ____ _____, according to the word of the Lord.

96. And Joshua the son Num was _____ ____ _____ _____ ____ _____; for Moses had laid his hands upon him: _____ _____ _____ ___ _____ hearkened unto him, and did as the Lord commanded Moses.

97. And there rose not a prophet since in Israel like unto _____, whom the Lord knew face to face.

The End DEUTERONOMY

THE NEW TESTAMENT

ST. MATTHEW

1. Abraham begat Isaac; and Isaac begat Jacob; and Jacob begat _____ _____ _____ _____ _____.

2. And Jacob begat Joseph the husband of Mary, of whom was born _____ who is called _____.

3. So all the generation from Abraham to David are _____ _____; and from David until the carrying away into Babylon are _____ _____; and from the carrying away into Babylon unto Christ are _____ _____.

4. Now the birth of Jesus Christ was on this wise; when as his mother Mary was espoused to Joseph, before they came together, _____ _____ _____ _____ _____ ____ _____ _____ _____.

5. Then Joseph her husband, _____ ____ _____ _____, and not willing to make her public example, was minded to put her away privily. But while he thought on these things, behold, the angel of the Lord appeared unto him in a dream, saying, Joseph, _____ _____ _____ _____, fear not to take unto thee Mary thy wife; for that which is conceived in her _____ _____ _____ _____ _____.

6. Now all this was done,` that it might be _____ which was spoken of the Lord by the Prophet saying, Behold, a virgin shall be with child, and shall bring forth a son, and they shall call his name _____, which being interpreted is, _____ _____ _____.

7. And knew her not til she had brought forth her _____

_____ and he   called his name   _____

8. Now when Jesus was born in _____ of Judaea in the days

of _____ the king, behold, there came wise men _____

_____   _____ to Jerusalem.

9. When Herod the king has heard these things, ___ _____ _____,

and all Jerusalem with him.

10. And being warned of God in a dream that they should _____ _____

_____   _____; they _____ into their own country

_____   _____.

11. And when they were departed, behold, _____ _____ ____

_____   _____ appeared to Joseph in a _____, saying,

arise, and take the young child and his mother and flee into Egypt, and be thou

there until I bring thee word; for Herod will seek the young child _____

_____   _____.

12. But when Herod was dead, behold, an angel of the Lord apeareth in a dream

to _____ _____ _____.   Saying, arise, and

take the young child and his mother and go into the land of Israel; for they are

dead which sought _____   _____   _____'s

_____.

13. But when he heard that Archelaus did reign in Judaea in the room of his

father Herod, he was afraid to go thither; notwithstanding _____

_____   ____ _____ ____ ___ _____, he

turned aside into the parts of Galilee. And he came and dwelt in a city called

_____; that it might be fulfilled which was spoken by the

prophets, He shall be called a _____.

14. In those days came John the Baptist _____ in the wilderness of _____.

15. For this is he that was spoken of by the Prophet Esaias, saying, _____ _____ ____ _____ _____ ____ _____ _____, prepare ye the way of the Lord, make his path straight.

16. And the same John had his raiment of camel's hair, and a leathern girdle about his loins; and his meat was _____ _____ _____ _____

17. I indeed baptize you with water unto repentance: but he that cometh after me is _____ _____ _____, whose shoes I am not worthy to bear; he shall baptize you with the _____ _____ _____ _____ _____.

18. Then cometh Jesus from Galilee to Jordan unto John to be _____ of him.

19. And Jesus, when he was baptized, went up straightway out of the water; and , _____, _____ _____ _____ _____ _____ _____, and he saw the Spirit of God descending _____ ____ _____, _____ _____ _____ _____. And lo a voice from heaven, saying, this is my beloved Son, _____ _____ ___ _____ _____ _____.

20. Then was Jesus led up of the Spirit into the wilderness to be tempted of the devil. And when he had fasted _____ _____ and _____ _____, he was afterward and hungered.

21. Jesus said unto him, it is written again, _____ _____ _____ _____ the Lord thy God.

91

22. Then saith Jesus unto him, Get thee hence, Satan: for it is written, _____

_____ _____ _____ _____ _____

_____, and him only shalt thou serve.

23.   Then the devil leaveth him, and behold, angels came and _____

_____ _____.

24. Now when Jesus had heard that John was _____ _____

_____ he departed into _____.

25. From that time Jesus began to preach, and to say, _____: for the
kingdom of heaven is at hand.

26. And he saith unto them, _____ _____, and I will make you
fishers of men.

27.   And going on from thence, he saw other two brethren, James the son
of Zebedee, and John his brother, in a ship with Zebedee their father, mending
their nets; and he called them. And they _____ left the ship
and their father and _____ _____.

28. And Jesus went about all Galilee, teaching in their synagogues and preaching
the gospel of the kingdom, and _____ all manner of sickness and
all manner of _____ among the people.

29. And seeing the multitudes, he went up into a _____: and
when he was set, his _____ came unto him: and he opened
his mouth, and taught them, saying,

30. Blessed are the poor in spirit; for theirs is the _____ _____
_____.

31. Blessed are the merciful; for they shall obtain _____.

32.   Blessed are ye, when men shall revile you and persecute you, and shall say all _____ ____ _____ _____ _____

_____, for my sake.

33. Verse _____ notes, Let your light so shine before men, that they may see your good works, and _____ your father which is in heaven.

34. Verse _____ says… but whosoever shall say, thou fool, shall be in danger of hell fire.

35. Verse _____ notes, But I say unto you, swear not at all; neither by heaven; for it is _____'s _____.

36.   That ye may be the children of your Father which is in heaven;   for he

_____ _____ _____ ____ _____ _____ _____

_____ and on the good, and sendeth rain on the _____ _____

_____ _____ _____.

37. Verses _____ entails "The Lord's Prayer".

38.   No man can serve two masters;   for either he will hate the one, and love the other;   or else he will hold to the one, and despise the other. _____

_____ _____ _____ _____ _____.

39. But _____ ye first the kingdom of God, and his _____; and all these things shall be _____ unto you.

40. Judge _____ , that ye be not judged.

41. Ask, and it shall be _____ you, _____, and ye shall find; _____, and it shall be opened unto you .

42. Beware of false prophets, which come to you in sheep's clothing, but inwardly they are _____ _____.

43. Wherefore by their _____ ye shall know them.

44. And the rain descended, and the _____ _____. And the
_____ _____, and beat upon that house; and ____ _____:
and great was the fall of it.

45. And Jesus said unto the Centurion, go thy way; and as thou hast
_____, so be it done unto thee. And his servant was healed in the
_____ _____.

46. And when he was entered into a ship, his disciples _____
_____ and behold, there arose a great _____ ____ ____
___, insomuch that the ship was _____ _____ _____
_____; but he was asleep. And his disciples came to him, and awoke
him, saying, _____, _____ ____: _____ _____.
And he saith unto them, why are ye fearful, ____ _____ _____
_____ _____. Then he arose, and rebuked the winds and the
sea; and there was a _____ _____. But the men marveled,
saying, _____ _____ ____ _____ ____
_____, that even the winds and the sea _____ _____!

47. And, behold, they brought to him a man sick of the palsy, lying on a bed;
and Jesus _____ _____ _____ said unto
the sick of the palsy; son, be of good cheer; _____ _____ ____
_____ _____.

48. And as Jesus passed forth from thence, he saw a man called _____,
sitting at the receipt of custom: and he said unto him _____
_____ and he arose, and _____ _____.

49. But go ye and learn what that meaneth, I will have mercy, and not sacrifice:
for I AM not come to call the righteousness, _____ _____
____ _____.

An Invitation To Know Him

50. While he spake these things unto them, behold, _____ _____
___ _____ _____, and worship him, saying, my
daughter is even _____ _____ but come and lay thou hand upon her,
and _____ _____ _____. And Jesus arose, and followed him,
and so did his disciples. And behold, a woman, which was diseased with ____
_____ ____ _____ _____ _____ came
behind him, and touched the hem of his garment: for she said within herself,
if I may touch his garment, I shall be whole. But Jesus turned him about, and
when he saw her, he said, daughter, be of good comfort; _____ _____
_____ _____ _____ _____. And the woman was
made whole from that hour.

51. And when Jesus came into the ruler's house, and saw the minstrels and
the people making a noise. He said unto them, give place, for the maid is not
dead, _____ _____. And they laughed him to scorn. But
when the people were put forth, he went in and took her by the hand, _____
_____ _____ _____.

52. And the fame hereof went aboard into _____ _____ ____.

53. And when he was come into the house, _____ _____
_____ came to him; and Jesus saith unto them, _____
____ _____ ___ _____ _____ ____ ____
_____? They said unto him yea Lord. Then _____
he their eyes saying, _____ ___ _____
_____ be it unto you. And their eyes were _____;
And Jesus straitly charged them saying, see that no man know this.

54. As they went out, behold, they brought to him a _____ _____
possessed with a devil. And when the devil was cast out, _____ _____
_____: and the multitudes marveled, saying, it was never so seen
in Israel.

55. And when Jesus had called unto him his twelve disciples, he gave
_____ _____ against unclean spirits, to cast them out,
and to _____ _____ _____ _____
_____ _____ _____ _____
_____ _____.

56. Now the names of the twelve apostles are these:

1. (a) _____ 7. (g) _____

2. (b) _____ 8. (h) _____

3. (c) _____ 9. (I)_____

4. (d) _____ 10. (j)_____

5. (e) _____ 11. (k)_____

6. (f) _____ 12. (l)_____

57. And as ye go, _____, saying, the kingdom of heaven is at
hand. Heal the sick, cleanse the lepers, and raise the dead, cast out devils:
_____ ____ _____ _____, _____
_____.

58. And whosoever shall not receive you, nor hear your words, when ye depart
out of that house or city, _____ _____ _____ _____
____ _____ _____.

59. But when they deliver you up, take _____ _____ how or
what ye shall speak; for it shall _____ _____ you in that same
hour what ye shall speak.

60. For it is not ye that speak, but the _____ ____ _____
_____ which speaketh _____ _____.

61. Fear them not therefore; for there is _____ _____,
that shall not be _____; and hid, that shall not _____
_____.

62. He that receiveth you receiveth me, and he that receiveth me _____
_____ _____ _____ _____.

63. And it came to pass, when Jesus had made an end of commanding his
_____ _____, he departed thence to _____
and to _____ in their cities.

64. Now when John had heard in the prison the works of Christ, he sent _____
_____ _____ _____.

65. And as they departed, Jesus began to say unto the multitudes _____
_____, what went ye out into the wilderness to see? A reed shaken with
the wind?

66. For this is he, of whom it is written, behold, I send my _____
before thy face, which shall _____ thy way before thee.

67. And from the days of _____ _____ _____
until now the kingdom of heaven suffered violence, and the violent take it by
force.

68. For all the prophets and the law _____ until
_____.

69. For my yoke is easy, and _____ _____ _____ _____.

70. And behold, there was a man which had his hand withered. And they asked
him, saying, _____ _____ _____ _____ _____
_____ _____ _____ _____? That they might accuse
him. And he said unto them, what man shall there be among you, that shall have
one sheep, and _____ _____ _____ _____ ___ _____

_____ _____ _____ _____, will he not lay hold on it, and lift it out? How much then is a man better than a sheep? Wherefore,

_____ _____ _____ _____ _____ _____ _____ _____

_____ _____. Then said he to the man, _____

_____ _____ _____. And he stretched it forth; and it was stored whole, like as the other.

71. He that is not with me is _____ _____; and he that _____ _____ with me scattered abroad.

72. Therefore I say unto you, all manner of sin and blasphemy _____ _____ _____ unto men: but the blasphemy _____ _____ _____ _____ shall not be forgiven unto men.

73. But I say unto you, that _____ _____ _____ that men shall speak, they _____ _____ _____ _____ in the day of judgement.

74. And he spake many things unto them in _____ , saying, behold, a sower went forth to sow; and when he sowed, some seeds _____ _____ _____ _____ _____, and the fowls came and devoured them up.

75. The sower sowed seeds in four different places; _____ _____ _____ _____, _____ _____, _____ _____ and _____ _____.

76. But he that received seed into the _____ _____ is he that heareth the word, and understand it; which also beareth fruit, and bringeth forth, some an _____, some _____, some _____.

77. Let both grow together until the harvest; and in the time of harvest I will say to the reaper, _____ ____ _____ _____ _____ _____, and bind them in bundles to burn them; but gather the wheat into my barn.

78. Then Jesus sent the multitude away, and went into the house; and his _____ came unto him, saying, declare unto us the _____ of the tares of the field. He answered and said unto them, he that soweth the good seed is the _____ ____ _____; the field is _____ _____; the good seed are the children of the _____; but the tares are the children of the _____ _____. The enemy that sowed them is _____ _____; the harvest is the _____ ____ _____ _____; and the reapers are _____ _____.

79. So shall it be at the end of the _____; the angels shall come forth, and _____ _____ _____ _____ _____ _____ _____.

80. For John said unto him, it is _____ _____ for thee to have _____.

81. And he sent, and _____ John in the _____.

82. And he commanded the multitude to sit down on the grass, and _____ _____ _____ _____ and the _____ _____, and looking up to heaven, he blessed, and brake, and gave the loaves to his _____, and the disciples to the multitude. And they did all eat and were filled; and they took up of the fragments that remained _____ _____ full. And they that had eaten were about _____ _____ _____ beside women and children.

83. And in the fourth watch of the night Jesus went unto them, _____ ____ _____ _____. And when the disciples saw him walking on the

sea, they were troubled, saying _____ _____ ___ _____; and they cried out for fear. But straightway Jesus spake unto them, saying, be of good cheer; _____ _____ ___ be not afraid. And Peter answered him and said, Lord, if it be thou, bid me to _____ unto thee on the water. And he said, _____. And when Peter was come down out of the ship, he walked on the water, to go to Jesus. But when he saw the wind boisterous, he was _____; and beginning to sink, he cried, saying, Lord, save me. And _____ Jesus stretched forth his hand, and caught him, and said unto him, O thou of little _____, wherefore didst thou doubt?

84. And besought him that they might only _____ the hem of his garment; as many as touched _____ _____ _____ _____.

85. Not that which goeth into the mouth defileth a man; but that which cometh out of _____ _____, this defileth a man.

86. Do not ye yet understand, that whatsoever entereth in at the mouth goeth into the belly, and is cast out into the draught? But those things which _____ _____ _____ _____ _____ come forth _____ ___ _____; and they defile the man. For out of _____ _____ proceed evil thoughts, murders, adulteries, fornications, thefts, false witness, blasphemies; these are the things which _____ ___ _____; but to eat with unwashen hands defileth _____ a man.

87. Then Jesus answered and said unto her, O woman, _____ ___ _____ _____; be it unto thee even as thou wilt. And her daughter was made whole from that very hour.

88. And they said, some say thou art _____ _____ _____: some, _____; and others, _____, or one of the prophets. He saith unto them, but whom say ye that ___ _____?

89. For the Son of man shall come in the glory of his Father _____ _____ _____; and then he _____ _____ _____ _____ according to his works.

90. While he yet spake, behold a bright cloud overshadowed them: and behold a voice out of the cloud, which said, this is my beloved Son, in whom I am well pleased; _____ _____ _____.

91. And while they abode in Galilee, Jesus said unto them, The Son of man shall be _____ into the hands of men: and they shall _____ _____, and the _____ _____ he shall be _____ _____. And they were exceeding sorry.

92. For the Son of man is come to save that which was lost. How think ye? If a man have an hundred sheep, and one of them be gone astray, doth he not leave the _____ _____ _____, and goeth into the mountains, and seeketh that which is gone astray? And if so be that he find it, verily I say unto you, he rejoiceth more of _____ sheep, than of the ninety and nine which went not astray.

93. Again I say unto you, that if two of you shall agree on earth as _____ _____ _____ that they shall ask, it shall be done for them of my father which is in heaven. For where _____ ____ _____ are gathered together in my name, there am I in the _____ of them.

94. Then came Peter to him and said, Lord, how oft shall my brother sin against me and I forgive him? Till seven times? Jesus saith unto him I say not unto thee, Until seven times; but Until _____ _____ _____.

95. And again I say unto you, it is easier for a camel to go through _____ _____ ____ ___ _____, than for a rich man to enter into the _____ _____ _____.

96. So the last shall be first, and first last: for many be called but _____

_____.

97. Even as the Son of man came not to be ministered unto, _____ ____

_____, and to give his life a ransom _____ _____.

98. So Jesus had _____ on them, and touched their eyes:
and immediately their eyes received sight, and they _____

_____.

99. Jesus sent two disciples saying unto them, go into the village over against
you, and straightway ye shall find an ass tired and a colt with her _____

_____, and bring them unto me. And if any man say aught unto you
ye shall say, _____ _____ _____ _____ ____

_____; and straightway he will send them, all this was done that it
might be fulfilled which was spoken by the prophet saying, _____ ____

_____ _____ ____ _____ _____, thy
king cometh unto thee, meek, and sitting upon an ass.

100. And Jesus went into the temple of God, and _____ _____ all them
that sold and brought in the temple, and overthrew the _____ ____

_____ _____, and the seats of them that sold doves.
And said unto them, it is written, my house shall be called the _____

____ _____, but ye have made it a den of thieves.

101. And when he saw a fig tree in the way, he came to it , and found nothing
thereon, but leaves only, and said unto it, let no fruit grow in thee henceforward
_____ _____. And presently the fig tree withered away. And when
the disciples saw it, they marvelled, saying, how soon is the fig tree withered
away! Jesus answered and said unto them, Verily I say unto you, if ye have
_____, and _____ _____, ye shall not only do
this which is done to the fig tree, but also if ye shall say unto this mountain,
____ _____ _____, and be thou cast into the sea; ____

_____ ____ _____. And all things, whatsoever ye shall ask in

prayer _____, ye shall receive.

102. They say unto him, Caesar's. Then saith he unto them, Render therefore unto Caesar the things which are Caesar's ; and unto God the _____

_____ _____ _____'s.

103. Now there were with us seven brethren; and the first, when he had married a wife, deceased, and having no issue, _____ _____

_____ _____ _____ _____. Likewise the second also, and the third unto the _____. And last of all the woman died also. Therefore in the resurrection whose wife shall she be of the seven? For they all had her.   Jesus answered and said unto them, _____ _____

_____, not knowing the scriptures, nor the _____ ____

_____. For in the resurrection they _____ _____,

_____ _____ _____ _____ _____ _____, but are as the angels of God in heaven.

104. Master, which is the great commandment in the law? Jesus said unto him, Thou shalt love _____ _____ _____ _____ with all thy heart, and with all thy soul, and with all thy mind. This is the first and great commandment. And the second is like unto it   Thou shalt _____

_____ _____ _____ _____. On these two commandments _____ all the law and the prophets.

105. And call no man your father upon the earth;   for one is your father,

_____ ____ ____ _____.

106. For I say unto you,   ye shall not see me henceforth,   till ye shall say,

_____ ____ ____ that cometh in the name of the Lord.

107. And as he sat upon the mount of Olives, the discipled came unto him privately, saying, _____ _____, _____ _____

_____ _____ _____? And what _____ _____ the signs of thy coming, and of the end of the world?

108. And ye shall hear of wars and rumours of wars: _____ _____ ____ _____ _____ _____; for all these things must come to pass, but the _____ ____ _____ _____ _____.

109. But he that shall endure unto the end, _____ _____ _____ _____ _____.

110. And this gospel of the kingdom shall be preached in _____ _____ _____ for a witness unto all nations; _____ _____ _____ _____ _____ _____.

111. For as the lightning cometh out of the _____, and shineth even unto the _____; so shall also the coming of the Son of man be.

112. And then shall appear the sign of the Son of man in heaven; and then shall all the _____ of the earth mourn, and they shall see the Son of man coming in the _____ ____ _____ with power and _____ _____.

113. Heaven and earth shall pass away, but my words _____ _____ _____ _____.

114. And knew not until the flood came, and took them all away; so shall also the _____ of the Son of man be.

115. Watch therefore; for ye know not _____ _____ your Lord doth come.

116. And the foolish said unto the wise, give us of your oil; for our lamps are _____ _____. But the wise answered, saying, not so; lest there be not enough for us and you; but go ye rather to them that sell, _____ _____

_____ _____. And while they went to buy, the _____ _____ _____; and they that were ready went in with him to the marriage; and _____ _____ _____ _____. Afterward came also the other virgins, saying, Lord, _____, _____ _____ _____.

117. His lord said unto him, well done, thou good and faithful servant; thou hast been _____ over a few things, I will make thee _____ over many things; enter thou into _____ _____ ____ _____ _____.

118. And these shall go away into _____ punishment; but the righteous into _____ _____.

119. And it came to pass, when Jesus had finished all these sayings, he said unto his disciples; ye know that after two days is the feast of the _____, and the Son of man is betrayed to be _____. There came a woman having an alabaster box of _____ _____ _____, and poured it on his head, as he sat at meat. But when his disciples saw it, they had indignation, saying , _____ _____ _____ _____ _____ _____? Verily, I say unto you _____ this gospel shall be _____ in the whole world, there shall also this, that this woman hath done, ____ _____ _____ ___ _____ ____ _____. Then one of the twelve, called _____ _____, went unto the chief priests, and said unto them, what will ye give me, and I will deliver him unto you? And they _____with him for _____ _____ ____ _____.

120. And as they did eat, he said, Verily I say unto you that one of you _____ _____ _____.

121. And as they were eating, Jesus took bread, and _____ _____,
and brake it and gave it to the disciples, and said, take, eat, this is _____
_____. And he took the cup, and _____ _____, and
gave it to them, saying, drink ye _____ _____ _____.

122. Jesus said unto him, verily I say unto thee, that this night, before the cock
crow, thou shall _____ _____ _____.

123. And while he yet spake, lo, Judas, one of the twelve, came, and with him
a _____ _____ with swords and staves, from
the chief priests and elders of the people. Now he that betrayed him gave them
a sign, saying, _____ ____ _____ _____,
that same is he; hold him fast.   And forthwith he came to Jesus, and said, Hail,
master; and kissed him.

124. And after a while came unto him they that stood by, and said to Peter, surely
thou also art one of them; _____ _____ _____
_____ _____. Then began he to _____ ____
____ _____, saying, I know not the man. And immediately the
_____ _____.   And Peter remembered the _____ ____
_____, which said unto him before the cock crow, thou shall deny
me thrice.   And he went out and _____ _____.

125. When the morning was come, all the chief priest and elders of the people
took counsel against Jesus to put him to _____. And when they had
bound him, they led him away, and delivered him to Pontius Pilate, _____
_____. Then Judas, which had betrayed him, when he saw that
he was _____, _____ _____,
and brought again the thirty pieces of silver to the chief priest and elders, saying
I have sinned in that I have betrayed _____ _____
_____.   And they said, what is that to us? See thou to that.   And

he casted down the pieces of silver in the temple, and departed and went and

_____   _____.

126.   When Pilate saw that he could prevail nothing, but that rather a tumult was made, he _____   _____,   _____   _____

_____   _____   before the multitude saying, I am innocent of the blood of this _____   _____; see ye to it.

127. Now from the _____   _____   there was darkness over all the land unto the _____   _____ .

128. And about the ninth hour Jesus cried with a loud voice, saying, Eli, Eli lama sabachthan? That is to say, _____   _____,   _____   _____

_____   _____   _____?

129. Jesus, when he had cried again with a loud voice, _____

_____   _____   _____ .

130. And the angel answered and said unto the women, fear not ye; for I know that ye _____   _____,   which was crucified. _____   _____

_____   _____: _____   _____   _____   _____,   as

he said.   Come, see the place where the Lord lay.

131. And as they went to tell his disciples, behold, Jesus met them, saying, _____   _____ . And they came and held him by the feet, and worshipped him.   Then said Jesus unto them, Be not afraid; go tell my brethren that they go into Galilee, _____   _____   _____   _____

_____   _____.

132.   Then the eleven disciples went away into Galilee, into a mountain where Jesus _____   _____   _____. And when they saw him, they worshipped him: _____   _____   _____ .

133. And Jesus came and spake unto them, saying, ALL POWER IS GIVEN UNTO ME ____ _____ _____ ____ _____.

Go ye therefore, and teach all nations, _____ them in the name of the Father, and of the Son, and of the Holy Ghost: Teaching them to observe all things _____ I have commanded you; and, lo, ___ _____ _____ _____ _____, EVEN UNTO THE END OF THE WORLD. AMEN.

THE END ST. MATTEW

ST. MARK

1. The beginning of the gospel of Jesus Christ, the son of God; as it is written in the prophets: _____, ___ __ _____ _____ _____ before thy face, which shall prepare thy way before thee.

2. The voice of one crying in the wilderness, _____ ____ _____ _____ _____ _____ _____, make his path straight.

3. John did baptize in the wilderness, and preached the baptism of _____ _____ _____ _____ _____ _____ _____.

4. And preached, saying, there cometh _____ _____ _____ _____ after me, the latchet of whose shoes I am not worthy to _____ _____ _____ _____.

5. I indeed have baptized you with water; but he shall baptize you _____ _____ _____ _____.

6. And it came to pass in those days, that Jesus came from Nazareth of Galilee, and was baptized of in _____. And straightway coming up out of the water, he saw the _____ _____, _____ _____ _____ _____ _____ _____ descending upon him. And there came a voice from heaven , saying, _____ _____ _____ _____ _____, in whom I am well pleased. And immediately the Spirit driveth him in the _____. And he was there in the wilderness _____ _____, tempted of _____; and was with the wild beasts; and the angel ministered unto him. Now after that John was _____ _____ _____ Jesus came into Galilee, _____ _____ _____ of the kingdom of God.

7. And saying, the time is fulfilled,   and the kingdom of   God is at hand: _____ _____, _____ _____ _____ _____.

8. Now as he walked by the sea of _____, he saw Simon and Andrew his brother casting a net into the sea; for they were fishers. And Jesus said unto them, _____ _____ _____ _____, and I will make you _____ _____ _____ _____ _____. And straightway they forsook their nets and _____ _____.

9. And there was in their synagogue a man with an _____ _____ and he cried out, saying, _____ _____ _____; what have we to do with thee, thou Jesus of Nazareth? Art thou come to destroy us? _____ _____ _____ who thou art, the Holy One of God. And Jesus rebuked him, saying, _____ _____ _____ _____ _____ _____ ____ _____. And when the unclean spirit _____ _____ _____, and cried with a loud voice, he came out of him.

10. And Jesus moved with _____ , put forth his hand, and touched him, and saith unto him, ___ _____: _____ _____ _____ .

11. And saith unto him, see thou say nothing to any man; but go thy way, _____ _____ _____ _____ _____ . And offer for thy cleansing those things which Moses commanded _____ _____ _____ _____ _____ .

12. And when they could not come nigh unto him for the press, they _____ _____ _____ where he was; and when they had broken it up, they let down the bed wherein _____ _____ _____ _____ _____ _____ , when Jesus saw _____ _____ , he said unto the sick of the palsy, son thy sins be forgiven thee.

13. And immediately when Jesus _____ _____ _____ _____ that they so reasoned within themselves, he said unto them, why reason ye these things in your _____? Whether is it easier to say to the sick of the palsy, thy sins be forgiven thee; or to say, Arise, and take up thy bed, and walk? But that ye may know that the _____ _____ _____ hast power on earth to _____ _____ (he saith to the sick of the palsy) I say unto thee, arise, and _____ _____ _____ _____ , and go thy way into thine house. And _____ he arose, took up the bed, and went forth before them all; insomuch that they were all amazed, and glorified God, saying, we never saw it on this fashion.

14. When Jesus heard it, he saith unto them: they that are _____ have no need of the _____ , but they that are sick: I came not to call the righteous, but _____ _____ _____ .

15. And he said unto them, the _____ was made for man, and not man for the _____ : Therefore, the Son of man is Lord also of the _____ .

16. And they watched him, whether he would heal him on the Sabbath day that they _____ _____ _____.

17. And when he had looked round about on them with anger, being grieved for the _____ _____ _____ _____, he saith unto the man, stretch forth thine hand. And his hand was _____ _____ as the other.

18. And unclean spirits, when they saw him _____ _____ _____ _____, and cried, saying, thou art the Son of God.

19. And he ordained twelve, that they should be with him, and that he might send them forth to _____, and to have _____ to heal sicknesses, and to cast out devils.

20. And he called them unto him, and said unto them in parables, how can _____ _____ _____ _____?

21. And if a house be divided against itself, that house _____ _____.

22. But he that shall blaspheme against the _____ _____ hath never forgiveness, but is in danger of _____ _____.

23. For whosoever shall do the will of God, the same is my brother, and my sister, and _____.

24. Hearken, behold, there went out a _____ _____ _____.

25. And he said unto them, know ye not this parable? And how then will ye know all _____.

26. The sower soweth the _____.

27. But when it is sown, it growth up and becometh _____ than all herbs, and shooteth out _____ _____ so that the fowls of the air may lodge under the _____ of it.

28. And he arose, and rebuked the wind, and said unto the sea, _____,
_____ _____, and the wind ceased, and there was a great calm.

29. For he said unto him, come out of the man,   thy unclean spirit and he
asked him _____ ____ _____ _____? And he
answered, saying, my name is _____ : for we are many.

30. And forthwith Jesus gave them leave, and the unclean spirits went out and
_____ _____ _____ _____: and the herd
ran violently down a steep place into the sea, (they were about two thousand)
and were _____ _____ _____ _____.

31. Howbeit Jesus suffered him not, but saith unto him, go home to thy friends,
and tell them _____ _____ _____ _____
_____ _____ _____, _____ _____, and hath
had _____ on thee.

32. And Jesus went with him and much people followed him, and thronged him.
And a certain woman which had an _____ ____ _____
_____ years, and had suffered many things of many physicians,
and _____ _____ _____ _____ _____ _____,
and was nothing bettered, but rather grew worse. When she had heard of
Jesus, came in the press behind, and touched his garment. For she said, _____
_____ _____ _____ but his clothes, I shall be whole. And
straightway the _____ ____ _____ _____
_____ _____ _____; and she felt in her body that she was
_____ of that plague. And Jesus immediately knowing in himself
that virtue had gone out of him, turned him about in the press, and said, _____
_____ _____ _____? And his disciples said unto
him, thou seest the multitude thronging thee and sayest thou, who touched me?
And he looked round about to see her that had done this things, but the woman
fearing and trembling, knowing what was done in her, _____ _____

_____ _____ _____ _____, and told him all the
truth. And he said unto her, daughter, _____ _____ _____
_____ _____ _____; go in peace, and be whole of
thy plague.

33. And whosoever shall not receive you, nor hear you, when ye depart thence,
_____ __ _____ _____ _____
_____ _____ ____ __ _____
_____ _____. Verily I say unto you, it shall be more tolerable for
Sodom and Gomorrha in the of judgement, than for that city.

34. But when Herod heard thereof, he said ____ ____ _____,
_____ ___ _____: he is risen from the dead.

35. For John had said unto Herod, it is not lawful for thee to have _____
_____'s _____.

36. And she went forth, and said unto her mother, what shall I ask? And she
said, _____ _____ _____ _____ _____
_____.

37. And brought his head in a charger, and gave it to the damsel; and the damsel
_____ _____ _____ _____ _____.

38. He saith unto them, how many loaves have ye? Go and see. And when they
knew, they say, _____ _____ _____ _____.

39. And they did all eat and were _____.

40. And they that did eat of the loaves were about _____ _____
_____.

41. And when even was come, the ship was in the _____ ____
_____ _____, and he alone on the land.

42. But when they saw him walking upon the sea, they supposed it had been
_____ _____, and cried out: for they all saw him, and was troubled.
_____ _____ _____ _____ _____
_____, and saith unto them, be of good cheer: _____ _____ _____;
be not afraid.

43. There is nothing from without a man, that entering into him _____
_____ _____; but the things which _____ _____
_____ _____, those are they that defile the man.

44. If any man have ears to hear, _____ _____ _____.

45. And were beyond measure astonished, saying, he hath done all things well:
_____ _____ _____ _____ _____ _____
_____, _____ _____ _____ _____ _____.

46. And he sighed deeply in his spirit, and saith, why doth this generation seek
after a sign? Verily I say unto you, there shall no sign be given _____
_____ _____.

47. And he took the blind man by the hand, and led him out of town; and when
he had spit on his eyes, and put his hands upon him, _____ _____
_____ _____ _____ _____ _____ and he looked
up, and said _____ _____ _____ _____ _____,
_____.   After that he put his hands again upon his eyes and made
him look up: and he was restored, _____ _____ _____ _____
_____. And he sent him away to his house, saying, neither go
into the town, nor tell it to any in the town.

48. And Jesus went out, and his disciples, into the towns of Caesarea Phillippi;
and by the way he asked his disciples, saying unto them, Whom do men say that
I am ?   And they answered, _____ _____ _____:
but some say, _____; and others, _____ _____ _____

_____. And he saith unto them, But whom say ye that I am? And Peter answered and saith unto him, _____ _____ _____ _____.

49. And when he had called the people unto him with his disciples also, he said unto them, _____ _____ _____ _____ _____, let him deny himself, _____ _____ _____ _____ _____, _____ _____ _____.

50. And after six days Jesus taketh with him Peter, and James and John and leadeth them up into an high mountain apart by themselves: and _____ _____ _____ _____ _____. And there appeared unto them _____ with _____ and they were _____ _____ _____.

51. And as they came down from the mountain, he charged them they should tell no man what things they had seen, till the _____ ____ _____ _____ _____ _____ _____ _____.

52. And one of the multitude answered and said, _____, I have brought unto thee my son, _____ _____ ___ _____ _____; and wheresoever he taketh him, ____ _____ _____; and he foamed, and gnasheth with his teeth, and pineth away; and I spake to thy disciples that they should cast him out; _____ _____ _____ _____.

53. And he asked his father, How long is it ago since this came unto him? And he said, ____ ___ _____. And oftimes it hath cast him into the _____, and into the _____, to destroy him; but if thou canst do any thing, _____ _____ ____ _____, _____ _____ ____. Jesus said unto him, if thou canst believe, _____ _____ ____ _____ ____ _____ _____ _____. And straightway the father of the child cried out, and

said with tears, Lord, I believe; _____ _____ _____ _____.
When Jesus saw that the people came running together, he rebuked the foul
spirit, saying unto him _____ _____ _____ _____

_____, I charge thee, come out of him, and _____ _____

_____ _____ _____. And the spirit cried, and rent him sore,

and _____ _____ _____ _____ and he was as one dead ;
insomuch that many said, he is dead. But Jesus took him by the hand, and lifted
him up and he arose. And when he was come into the house, his disciples asked
him privately, Why _____ _____ we cast him out? And
he said unto them, this _____ can come forth by nothing, but by

_____ _____ _____.

54. For he taught his disciples, and said unto them, the Son of man is delivered
into the hands of men, and they shall kill him; and after that he is killed, he
shall _____ _____ _____ _____. But they
_____ _____ that saying, and were afraid to ask him.

55. But they held their peace; for by the way they had disputed among themselves,

_____ _____ _____ _____ _____.

56. Whosoever shall receive one of such children in my name, _____
_____ and whosoever shall receive me, receiveth not me, _____ _____
_____ _____ _____.

57. For he that is not against us ____ _____ _____ _____.

58. Where their worm dieth _____, and the fire is not _____.

59. And the Pharisees came to him and asked him, is it lawful for a man to
_____ _____ his wife? Tempting him. And he answered and
said unto them, what did _____ _____
_____?

60. And he saith unto them, whosoever shall put away his wife and marry another, committeth _____ _____ _____.
And if a woman shall put away her husband, and be married to another, she committeth _____.

61. But when Jesus saw it, he was much displeased, and said unto them, suffer the little children to come unto me, and _____ _____ _____; for of such is the kingdom of God. Verily I say unto you, whosoever shall not receive the kingdom of God as a little child, he shall not enter therein. And he took them up in his arms, put his hands upon them, and _____ _____.

62. It is easier for a camel to go through the eye of a needle, than for _____ _____ _____ to enter into the kingdom of God.

63. And Jesus looking upon them saith, with men it is _____, but not with God: for with God _____ _____ _____ _____.

64. They said unto him, _____ _____ _____ that we may sit, _____ on the thy right hand, and the _____ on thy left hand, in thy glory.

65. For even the Son of man came not to be ministered unto, but to minister, and to give his life _____ _____ _____ _____.

66. And Jesus said unto him, go thy way; _____ _____ _____ _____ _____ _____. And immediately he received his sight, and followed Jesus in the way.

67. And Peter calling to remembrance saith unto him, Master, behold, the fig tree which thou cursedst is withered away. And Jesus answering saith unto them, _____ _____ _____ _____. For verily I say

unto you, that whosoever shall say unto this mountain, be thou removed, and be thou cast into the sea, and _____ _____ _____ ____ _____ _____, but shall believe that those things which he saith shall come to pass; he _____ _____ _____ _____ _____. Therefore I say unto you, what things soever ye desire, when ye pray, _____ that ye _____ _____, and ye shall have them.

68. And he began to speak unto them in parables. A certain man _____ ____ _____, and set an hedge about it, and digged a place for the winevat, and built a tower, and let it out to husbandmen, and went into a far country.

69. And Jesus answered him, The first of all the commandments is, Hear, O Israel; the Lord our God is one Lord: and thou shalt love the Lord thy God with all thy _____, and with all they _____, and with all thy _____, and with all thy _____: this is the first commandment. And the second is like, namely this, Thou shalt love thy _____ as thy thyself. There is none other commandment greater than these.

70. And the gospel must first be published among _____ _____

71. But when they shall lead you, and deliver you up, _____ _____ _____ beforehand what ye shall speak, neither do ye premeditate: but whatsoever shall be given you in that hour, that speak ye; for it is not ye that speak, _____ _____ _____ _____.

72. And then shall they see the Son of man coming in the clouds with great _____ _____ _____:

73. Heaven and earth shall pass away: but my words _____ _____ _____ _____.

74. But of that day and that hour knoweth no man, no, not the angels which are in heaven, neither the Son, _____ _____ _____.

75. And what I say unto you I say unto all, _____.

76. And Jesus said, _____ _____ _____ , why trouble ye her? She hath wrought a good work _____ _____.

77. And he sent forth two of his disciples and saith unto them, go ye into the city, and shall meet you a man bearing ____ _____ _____ _____ : follow him.

78. And he will show you a _____ _____ _____ furnished and prepared: there make ready for us.

79. And as they sat and did eat, Jesus said, verily I say unto you, one of you which eateth with me _____ _____ _____.

80. After the eating and drinking of the Last Supper, Jesus said unto them, this is my blood of the _____ _____ which is shed for many.

81. And when they had sung a hymn, they went out into the _____ _____ _____.

82. And Jesus saith unto him, verily I say unto thee, that this day, even in this night, before the cock crow twice, _____ _____ _____ _____ _____.

83. Watch ye and pray, lest ye enter into temptation, the _____ _____ ____ _____, but the flesh is weak.

84. And he cometh the third time, and saith unto them, _____
_____ _____, and take your rest: it is enough, _____ _____
____ _____: behold, the Son of man is betrayed into the hands of
sinners.

85. And Jesus said, I AM; and ye shall see the Son of man sitting on the
_____ _____ ____ _____ and coming in the
clouds of heaven.

86. And they cried out again, _____ _____.

87. And they clothed him _____ _____, _____
_____ ____ crown of thorns.

88. And they compel one Simon a Cyrenian, who passed by, coming out of the
country, the father of Alexander and Rufus _____ _____ _____
_____.

89. And they bring him unto the place Golgotha, which is being interpreted,
_____ _____ _____ ___ _____.

90. And they gave him to drink wine mingled with myrrh: but he received it
_____.

91. And when they had crucified him, they parted his garments, _____
_____ _____ _____, what every man should
take.

92. Likewise also the chief priests mocking said among themselves with the
scribes, he saved others, _____ _____ _____
_____.

93. And when the sixth hour was come, there was darkness over the whole land
until the _____ hour.

94. And Jesus cried with a _____ _____, and gave up the ghost.

95. And he saith unto them, be not affrighted: ye seek Jesus of Nazareth, which was crucified: _____ _____ _____; _____ _____ _____ _____: behold the place where they laid him.

96. Now when Jesus was risen early the first day of the week, he appeared first to _____ _____, out of whom he had cast _____ _____.

97. Afterward he appeared unto _____ _____ as they sat at meat, and upbraided them with their unbelief and hardness of heart, because they believed _____ _____ _____ _____ _____ _____ _____ _____ _____ _____.

98. And he said unto them: go ye into all the world, and _____ _ _____ _____ _____ _____ _____. He that _____ and is _____ shall be saved; but he that believeth not shall be damned. And these signs shall _____ _____ _____ _____ _____; in my name shall they _____ _____ _____; they shall speak with _____ _____. They shall _____ _____ _____ and if they drink any _____ _____, it shall not hurt them; they shall _____ _____ ___ ____ ___ ___, and they shall recover. So then after the Lord had spoken unto them, he was _____ _____ _____ _____ and _____ ____ _____ _____ _____ _____ _____. And they went forth, and preached every where, the Lord working with them and _____ _____ _____ _____ _____ _____.

THE END ST. MARK

1. And they were both righteous before God, walking in all the commandments and ordinances of the Lord, _____. And they had no child, because that Elisabeth _____ _____, and they both were now well stricken in years.

2. And there appeared unto him an angel of the Lord standing on the right side of the altar of incense. But the angel said unto him fear not Zacharias; for thy prayer is heard; and thy wife Elisabeth _____ _____ _____ ___ _____, and thou shalt call his name _____.

3. And Zacharias said unto the angel, whereby shall I know this? For I am an old man and my wife well stricken in years. And the angel answering said unto him, _____ _____ _____, _____ _____ _____ _____ _____ _____ _____ and am sent to speak unto thee, and to show thee these glad tidings. And behold, _____ _____ ____ _____ _____ _____ _____ ____ _____, until the day that these things shall be performed, because thou _____ _____ my words, which shall be fulfilled in their season. And when he came out he could not speak unto them and they perceived that he had seen a vision in the temple, for he beckoned unto them, and _____ _____.

4. And in the sixth month _____ _____ _____ was sent from God unto a city of Galilee, named Nazareth.

5. And the angel said unto her, fear not Mary; for thou hast found _____ _____ _____.

6. And, behold, thou shall conceive in thy womb, and bring forth a son, and shall call his name _____.

7. Then said Mary unto the angel, how shall this be, _____ _____

_____ _____ ____ _____?

8. And the angel answered and said unto her the Holy Ghost shall come upon

thee, and the _____ _____ _____ _____ shall

overshadow thee; therefore also that holy thing which shall be born of thee

shall be called _____ _____ ____ _____. And behold, thy

cousin _____, she hath also conceived a son in _____

_____ _____; and this is the sixth month with her, _____ ____

_____. For with God _____ _____ ____

_____.

9. And Mary said, behold the handmaid of the Lord; be it unto me _____

____ _____ _____.

10. And Mary said, my soul doth _____ the Lord.

11. Now Elisabeth's full time came that she should be delivered; and she brought

forth ____ _____.

12. And he asked for a writing table, and wrote, saying _____ _____

____ _____.

13.   And his mouth was opened immediately, and his tongue loosed and

____ _____, _____ _____ _____.

14. And the child grew, and waxed strong in spirit, and was in the deserts till the

day his _____ _____ _____.

15. And she brought forth her firstborn son, and wrapped him in _____

_____, and laid him in a manger; because there was no room for

them in the inn.

16. Glory to God in the hightest, and on earth peace, _____ _____
_____   _____.

17. And when eight days were accomplished for the _____
_____ _____ _____ , his name was called _____ ,
which was so named of the angel before he was _____ _____
_____ _____ .

18. And behold, there was a man in Jerusalem, whose name was Simeon; and the
same man was just and devout,   waiting for the consolation of Israel; _____
_____ _____ _____ _____ _____ _____ .
And it was revealed unto him by the Holy Ghost, that he should not _____
_____ ,   before he had seen the Lord's Christ.   And he _____
_____ _____ _____ into the temple; and when the parents
brought in the child Jesus, to do for him after the custom of the law, Then took
he him up in his arms, and _____ _____ , and said, Lord, now
lettest thou thy _____ _____ ____ _____ ,
according to thy word. For mine eyes have seen thy _____ .

19. Now his parent went to Jerusalem every year at the feast of the Passover, and
when he was _____ _____ _____ , they went
up to Jerusalem after the custom of the feast.

20. And when they had fulfilled the days, as they returned, the child _____
_____ in Jerusalem and Joseph and his mother _____
_____ _____ ____ .

21. And it came to pass, that after three days they found him in the temple,
_____ ____ _____ _____ _____ _____
_____ ,   both hearing them, and asking them questions.

22. And he said unto them, How is it that ye sought me? Wist ye not that _____

_____ _____ _____ _____ _____'s

_____.

23. And Jesus increased in wisdom and stature, and in _____

_____ _____ _____ _____.

24. Every valley shall be filled, and every mountain and hill shall be brought

low; and the crooked shall be made straight, and the rough ways shall be made

smooth; and all flesh _____ _____ _____

_____ _____ _____.

25. Then said he to the multitude that came forth to be _____

_____ _____, O generation of vipers, who hath warned you to flee from

_____ _____ _____ _____?

26. John answered, saying unto them all, I indeed baptize you with water;

_____ _____ _____ _____ ____ _____,

the latchet of whose shoes I am not worthy to unloose; he shall baptize you

with _____ _____ _____ _____ _____

_____.

27. Added yet this above all, that he shut up _____ _____

_____.

28. Now when all the people were baptized, it came to pass, that Jesus also being

baptized, and praying, the heaven was opened, and the Holy Ghost descended in

a bodily shape like a dove upon him, and ____ _____ _____

_____ _____, which said,   Thou art my beloved Son,

_____ _____ ____ _____ _____ _____.

29. And Jesus himself began to be about _____ _____

_____ _____.

30. And Jesus being full of _____ _____ _____ returned from Jordan, and was led by the spirit into the wilderness, being _____ _____ tempted by the devil. And in those days he did _____ _____; and when they were ended, he afterward hungered.

31. And when the devil had ended all the temptations, _____ _____ _____ _____ _____ ____ _____.

32. And he came to Nazareth, where he had been brought up: and as his custom was, he went into the synagogue _____ _____ _____ _____ and stood up to read. And there was delivered unto him _____ _____ ____ _____ _____ _____. And when he had opened the book, he found the place where it was written: _____ _____ ____ _____ _____ _____ _____ _____, because he hath anointed me to preach the gospel to the poor, he hath sent me to heal the brokenhearted, to preach deliverance to the captives and recovering of sight to the blind, to set at liberty them that are bruised, to preach, the acceptable year of the Lord. And he closed the book, and gave it back to the minister, and sat down. And the _____ ____ _____ _____ _____ _____ ____ _____ _____ were fastened on him. And he began to say unto them, this day is this scripture _____ _____ _____ _____.

33. And they were astonished at his doctrine _____ _____ _____ _____ _____ _____.

34. And they were all amazed, and spake among themselves, saying, what a word is this! For with _____ _____ _____ he commandeth the unclean spirits, and they come out.

35. And devils also came out of many, crying out, and saying, Thou art Christ the Son of God. And he rebuking them suffered them not to speak: _____

_____ _____ _____ _____ _____

_____.

36. And Simon answering said unto him, Master, _____ _____

_____ _____ _____ _____, _____

_ _____ _____ _____: nevertheless at

thy word I will let down the net. And when they had this done, they inclosed

____ _____ _____ ____ _____:

and their net brake.

37. And it came to pass on a certain day, as he was teaching, that there were

_____ _____ _____ ____ _____

_____ _____ _____, which were come out of

every town of Galilee, and Judaea, and Jerusalem: and the power of the Lord

_____ _____ ____ _____ _____.

38. And they that were vexed with unclean spirits; and _____ _____

_____ the whole multitude _____ _____

_____ _____ for there went virtue out of him, and healed

them all.

39. But I say unto you which hear, Love your enemies, ____ _____

____ _____ _____ _____ _____, Bless

them that curse you, and _____ _____ _____ which

despitefully use you.

40. But love ye your enemies, and do good, and lend, hoping for nothing again

_____ _____ _____ _____ ____ _____

and ye shall be the children of the Highest: for he is kind unto the unthankful

and to the evil.

41. Judge not, and ye shall not be judged. Condemn not and ye shall not be

condemned; forgive, _____ _____ _____ _____

_____.

42. And why call ye me, Lord, Lord, and do not the things which I say? Whosoever cometh to me, _____ _____ _____ _____, _____ _____ _____, I will show you to whom he is like: He is like a man which built an house and digged deep, and laid the foundation on a rock and when the flood arose, the stream beat vehemently upon that house, _____ _____ _____ _____ _____; for it was found upon a rock.

43. And when the Lord saw her, he had _____ on her, and said unto her, weep not.

44. For I say unto you, among those that are born of women there is not a breater prophet than _____ _____ _____; but he that is least in the kingdom of God is greater than he.

45. And, behold, a woman in the city, which was a sinner, when she knew that Jesus sat at meat in the Pharisee's house, brought an alabaster box of ointment, and stood at his feet behind him weeping, _____ _____ _____ _____ _____ _____ _____ _____, and did wipe them with the hairs of her head, and kissed his feet, and anointed them with the ointment.

46. And he said unto her, thy sins are _____.

47. And he said to the woman _____ _____ hath saved thee; go in peace.

48. Now the parable is this: the seed is the word of _____.

49. And Jesus said, somebody hath touched me: for I perceive that _____ _____ _____ _____ _____ _____.

50. But when Jesus heard it, he answered him saying, fear not _____ _____, and she shall be made whole.

51. Then he called his twelve disciples together, and gave them _____

_____ _____ over all devils, and to cure diseases.

52. And whosoever will not receive you, when ye go out of that city, shake

off the very dust from your feet _____ ____ _____

_____ _____.

53. For they were about five thousand men. And he said to his disciples make

them sit down by _____ _____ _____ _____.

54. And it came to pass, as he was alone praying, his disciples were with him;

and he asked them, saying, Whom say the people that I am? They answering

said, John the Baptist; but some say, Elias; and others say, that one of the old

prophets is risen again. He said unto them, _____ _____

_____ _____ _____ ___ _____? Peter answering said, The

Christ of God.

55. And he straitly charged them, and commanded them to tell _____ _____

_____ _____.

56. And behold, there talked with him two men, which were _____

_____ _____.

57. While he thus spake, there came a cloud, and overshadowed them and they

feared as they entered into the cloud. And there came a voice out of the cloud,

saying, This is my beloved Son: _____ _____.

58. And Jesus said unto him, forbid him not; for he that is _____

_____ _____ _____ _____ _____.

59. And Jesus said unto him, foxes have holes, and birds of the air have nests

but the Son of man hath _____ _____ _____ _____

_____ _____.

60. After these things the Lord appointed other _____ also, and sent them two and two before his face into every city and place, whither he himself would come. And unto the mission of the _____ he said; the harvest truly is great _____ _____ _____ _____ _____: pray ye therefore the Lord of the harvest, that he would send forth laborers into his harvest. Go your ways; behold, _____ _____ _____ _____ _____ _____ _____ _____.

61. And the seventy returned again with joy, saying, Lord even the devils are subject unto us _____ _____ _____. And he said unto them   I beheld Satan as lighting fall from heaven.   Behold, I give unto you _____ to tread on serpents and scorpions, and over all the _____ _____ _____ _____ and nothing shall by any means hurt you. Notwithstanding in this rejoice not, that the spirits are subject unto you; but rather rejoice, because _____ _____ _____ _____ _____ _____.

62. And behold, a certain lawyer stood up, and tempted him, saying, Master, _____ _____ ____ _____ _____ _____ _____ _____?   He said unto him, what is written in the law? How readest thou?

63. Which now of these three, thinkest thou, was neighbour unto him that _____ _____ _____ _____? And he said, he that showed mercy on him. Then Jesus said unto him _____ _____ _____ _____ _____.

64. But one thing is needful; and Mary _____ _____ _____ _____ _____, which shall not be taken away from her.

65. And it came to pass, that, as he was praying in a certain place, when he ceased, one of his disciples said unto him, _____, _____ _____ _____ _____, as John also taught his disciples.

66. And I say unto you _____, and it shall be given you _____, and ye shall find _____, and it shall be opened unto you. For every one that _____ receiveth, and he that _____ findeth, and to him that _____ it shall be opened.

67. He that is not with me is _____ me; and he that gathered not with me _____.

68. And as he spake, a certain Pharisee besougth him to dine with him; and he went in and _____ _____ ____ _____, and when the Pharisee saw it, he marveled that he had not _____ _____ _____ _____. And the Lord said unto him; now do ye Pharisees make clean the outside of the cup and the platter but your _____ _____ is full of _____ _____ _____.

69. For there is nothing covered, that shall not _____ _____; neither hid, that shall   not   _____ _____.

70. And whosoever shall speak a word against the Son of man it shall be _____ _____. But unto him that _____ against the _____ _____ it shall not be forgiven.

71. And when they bring you into the synagogues, and unto magistrates and powers,   take ye no thought how or what thing ye shall answer or what ye _____ _____. For the _____ _____ _____ _____ _____ in the same hour what ye ought to say.

72. But rather seek ye the kingdom of God and all these things shall _____

_____ _____ _____.

73. Be ye therefore ready also; for the Son of man cometh at an hour _____

_____ _____ _____.

74. And that servant, which knew his lord's will, and prepared not himself, neither did according to his will, shall be _____ _____

_____ _____.

75. And, behold, there was a woman which had ____ _____ ____

_____ eighteen years and was bowed together, and could in no wise _____ ____ _____. And Jesus saw her, he called her to him, and said unto her _____, _____ _____

_____ _____ _____ _____ and he laid his hands on her and immediately she was made straight and _____

_____.

76. And ought not this woman, being a daughter of Abraham, _____

_____ _____ _____, lo thou eighteen years, be loosed from this bond on the Sabbath day?

77. There shall be weeping and gnashing of teeth, when ye shall see _____ _____ _____ _____ _____, and all prophets, in the kingdom of God, and you yourselves thrust out.

78. And, behold, there are last which shall be first, and there are _____

_____ _____ _____ _____.

79. But when thou makest a feast, call the poor, the maimed, the lame, the blind, and thou shall be _____; for they cannot recompense thee; for thou shall be _____ _____

_____ _____ _____ _____ _____.

80. I say unto you, that likewise joy shall be in heaven over one _____

_____ _____, more than over ninety and nine just persons,

which need _____ _____.

81. Likewise, I say unto you, there is joy in the present of the _____

_____ _____ over one sinner that repenteth.

82. It was meet that we should make merry, and be glad; for this thy brother

was _____ and is alive again; and _____ _____ _____

_____ _____.

83. There was a certain rich man, which was clothed in _____

_____ _____ _____, and fared sumptuously _____

_____. And there was a certain begger named _____,

which was laid at his gate, full of sores, and desiring to be fed with the

_____ which fell from the rich man's table; moreover the dogs came and

licked his sores. And it came to pass, the begger died, and was _____

_____ _____ _____ _____ _____'s

_____; the rich man also died, and was buried; _____ _____

_____ _____ _____ _____ _____ _____, being

in torments, and seeth Abraham afar off, and Lazarus in his bosom. And he

cried and said Father Abraham have mercy on me, and send Lazarus, that he

may _____ _____ _____ _____ _____ _____

_____ _____ and cool my tongue, for I am tormented in this flame.

84. And he said unto him, if they hear not _____ _____ _____

_____ neither will they be persuaded, though one rose from the

dead.

85. Take heed to yourselves; if thy brother trespass against thee, rebuke him!

And if he repent, _____ _____.

86. And as he entered into a certain village, there met him _____ _____ that were lepers, which stood afar off.

87. And when he saw them, he said unto them, go show yourselves unto the priest, and it cam to pass, that, as they went, _____ _____ _____.

88. And one of them, when he saw that he was healed, _____ _____ and with a loud voice _____ _____.

89. And Jesus answering said were there not ten cleaned? _____ _____ _____ _____ _____ _____?

90. And he said unto him, arise, go thy way; thy _____ hath made thee whole.

91. Neither shall they say, lo here! Or lo there! For behold, the kingdom of God _____ _____ _____.

92. Remember Lot's _____.

93. And he said, the things which are impossible with men _____ _____ _____ _____.

94. And Jesus said unto him, receive thy sight _____ _____ _____ _____ _____.

95. And immediately he received his sight, and followed him, _____ _____ and all the people, when they saw it, gave praise unto God.

96. And Jesus said unto him, This day is salvation come to this house, forasmuch as he also is ____ _____ _____ _____. For the Son of man is come to seek and to save _____ _____ ____ _____.

97. And when he had thus spoken, he went before _____

____ ____ _____.

98. Saying, Blessed be the king that cometh in the name of the Lord,

_____ ____ _____, _____ _____ ____

_____ _____.

99. And some of the Pharisees from among the multitude said unto him, Master,

_____ _____ _____.

100. And he answered and said unto them, I tell you that, if these should hold

their peace, _____ _____ _____ _____

_____ _____.

101. Show me a penny. Whose image and superscription hath it? They answered

and said _____'s. And he said unto them, _____

_____ _____ _____ the things which be

Caesar's, and unto _____ _____ _____ _____

____ _____.

102. And the third took her; and in like manner the seven also: and they left no

children and died. Last of all the woman died also. Therefore in the resurrection,

_____ _____ ____ _____ ____ _____? For

seven had her to wife. And Jesus answering said unto them, the children

____ _____ _____ _____, and are given

in marriage. But they which shall be accounted worthy to obtain that world,

and the resurrection from the dead, _____ _____,

_____ _____ _____ ____ _____.

103. Heaven and earth shall pass away, but _____ _____ _____

_____ pass away.

104. Watch ye therefore, and _____ _____, that ye may be _____ _____ to escape all these things that shall come to pass, and to stand before the Son of man.

105. Now the feast of unleavened bread drew nigh, which is called _____ _____. And the chief priest and scribes sought how they might kill him; for they feared the people. Then entered _____ into Judas surnamed _____ being of the number of the _____. And he went his way and communed with the chief priest and captain, how he might betray him unto them. And they were glad, and _____ to give him money. And he promised and sought opportunity to betray him unto them on the absent of the multitude. Then came the day of unleavened bread, when the Passover must be killed. And he sent _____ _____ _____ saying, go and prepare us the Passover, that we may eat. And they said unto him, where wilt thou that we prepare? And he said unto them, behold, when ye are entered into the city, _____ _____ ____ _____ _____ _____, bearing a pitcher of water, follow him into the house where he entereth in. and ye shall say unto the Goodman of the house, the Master saith unto thee, _____ ____ _____ _____, where I shall eat the Passover with my disciples? And he shall show you a large upper room _____: there make ready.

106. And he took the cup, and gave thanks, and said, take this, and divide it among yourselves. For I say unto you, ____ _____ _____ _____ ____ _____ _____ ____ _____ _____, until the kingdom of God shall come. And he took bread, and gave thanks, and brake it, and gave unto them saying _____ ____ _____ _____ which is given for you; _____ ____ ____ _____ ____ _____. Likewise also the cup after supper, saying, this cup is the _____ _____ ____ _____ _____, which is shed for you.

136

107. And the Lord said, Simon, Simon, behold, Satan hath desired to have you, that he may sift you as wheat. But I have prayed for thee, that _____ _____ _____ _____ and when thou art converted, strengthen thy brethren.

108. And he said unto them, when I sent you without purse, and scrip, and shoes, lacked ye anything? And they said _____.

109. And when he was at the place, he said unto them pray that ye enter not _____ _____.

110. And while he ye spake, behold a multitude, and he that was called Judas, one of th twelve, went before them, and drew near unto Jesus to _____ _____. But Jesus said unto him, Judas betrayest thou the Son of man _____ ____ _____?

111. And one of them smote the servant of the high priest and _____ _____ _____ _____ _____. And Jesus answered and said suffer ye thus far. And he touched his ear, _____ _____ _____.

112. And the Lord turned, and looked upon Peter, and Peter remembered the word of the Lord, how he had said unto him, before the cock crow; thou shall deny me thrice. And Peter went out, and _____ _____

113. And the whole multitude of them arose, and led him unto _____.

114. Then he questioned with him in many words; _____ ____ _____ _____ _____.

115. And the same day, Pilate and Herod were made _____ _____ for before they were at enmity between themselves.

116. I will therefore chastise him, and _____ _____.

117. But they cried, saying, crucify him, _____ _____.

118. Then said Jesus, Father, forgive them; for they know not what they do. And they _____ _____ _____, _____ _____ _____.

119. And he said unto Jesus, Lord remember me when thou comest into thy kingdom. And Jesus said unto him, verily I say unto thee, _____ _____ _____ _____ _____ _____ _____ _____.

120. And when Jesus had cried with a loud voice, he said _____, _____ _____ _____ ___ _____ ____ _____: and having said thus, he gave up the ghost.

121. This man went unto Pilate, and begged the body of _____ and he took it down, and _____ _____ _____ _____, and laid it in a sepulchre that was hewn in stone, where _____ man before was laid.

122. And they returned, and prepared spices and ointments and _____ _____ _____ _____ _____ _____ _____ _____.

123. And they found the stone _____ _____ from the sepulchre.

124. And they entered in and found _____ the body of the Lord Jesus.

125. And it came to pass, as they were much perplexed thereabout, behold, two men stood by them in _____ _____.

126. He is not here, but is risen; remember how he spake unto you when he was yet in Galilee saying, the Son of man must be delivered into the hands of sinful

men, and be crucified, _____ _____ _____ _____

_____ _____.

127. And they remembered his _____.

128. Then arose Peter, and ran unto the sepulchre; and stooping down, he beheld
the _____ _____ _____ _____

_____, and departed, wondering in himself at that which was _____

____ _____.

129. And he said unto them, what things? And they said unto him, concerning
_____ ____ _____, which was a prophet
mighty in deed and word before God and all the people.

130. And when they found not his body, they came, saying that they had also
_____ ____ _____ ____ _____, which
said that he was _____.

131. But they constrained him, saying, abide with us; for it is toward evening,
and the day is far spent. And he went in _____ _____ _____

_____.

132. And their eyes were opened _____ _____ _____
_____; and he vanished out of their sight.

133. And he said unto them, why are ye troubled? And why do _____
_____ ____ _____ _____?

134. Behold, my hands and my feet, that it is I myself; handle me, and see; for
a _____ _____ _____ _____ _____

_____, as ye see me have.

135. And when he had thus spoke, he showed them _____ _____

_____ _____ _____.

136. Then opened he their understanding, that they might _____
_____ _____ _____.

137. And that repentance and remission of sins should be preached in his name among all nations, _____ _____ _____.
And ye are _____ of these things. And behold, I send the promise of my Father upon you; but tarry ye in the city of _____,
_____ _____ _____ _____ _____ _____
_____ _____ _____. And he led them out as far as to _____, and he lifted up his hands _____ _____
_____. And it came to pass, while he blessed them, he was parted from them and _____ _____ _____ _____. And they worshipped him, and returned to _____ with great joy. And were continually in the temple, _____ _____
_____ _____. AMEN.

THE END ST. LUKE

ST. JOHN

1. In the beginning was the _____ and the _____ was with God, and the _____ was God.

2. All things were made by _____; and without _____ was not any thing made _____ _____ _____.

3. In him was _____ and the _____ was the _____
_____ _____.

4. There was a man sent from _____ whose name was _____.

5. The same came for a witness, _____ _____ _____
of the Light, that all men through him might believe.

140

6. He was not that Light, but was sent to bear witness ____ _____
_____.

7. Which were born, not of blood, nor of the will of the flesh, nor of the will of
man, _____ ____ _____.

8. John bare witness of him, and cried, saying, this was he of whom I spake,
he that cometh after me is preferred before me: _____ _____ _____
_____ _____.

9. And John bare record, saying, I saw the _____ _____
_____ _____ like a dove, and it abode upon
him.

10. And I saw, and bare record that this ____ _____ _____ ____
_____.

11. And he saith unto him, verily, verily, I say unto you, hereafter ye shall ye
shall _____ _____ _____, and the angels of God
_____ _____ _____ upon
the Son of man.

12. And both Jesus was called, and his disciples, to the _____.

13. And when they wanted wine, the mother of Jesus saith unto him, _____
_____ _____ _____.

14. Jesus saith unto her, Woman, what have I to do with thee? _____
_____ ____ _____ _____ _____. His mother
saith unto the servants, whatsoever he saith unto you, _____ _____.

15. When the ruler of the feast had tasted the water, _____ _____
_____ _____, and knew not whence it was (but the servants

which drew the water knew) the governor of the feast called the _____

_____.

16. This beginning of miracles did Jesus in Cana of Galilee, and manifested forth his glory; and his _____ _____

_____ _____.

17. Jesus answered and said unto them, destroy this temple, and _____ _____ _____, I will raise it up.

18. But he spake of the temple of his _____.

19. But Jesus did not commit himself unto them, because he knew _____ _____. And needed not that any should testify of man: _____ _____ _____ _____ _____ _____ _____.

20. Nicodemus saith unto him, How can a man be born when he is old? Can he enter the second time into his mother's womb and be born? Jesus answered, verily, verily, I say unto thee, except a man be _____ _____ _____ _____ _____ _____ _____, _____ _____ enter into the kingdom of God. That which is born of the _____ ____ _____; and that which is born of the _____ ____ _____. Marvel not that I said unto thee, ____ _____ _____ _____ _____.

21. For God so loved the world, that he gave his only begotten Son, that whosoever _____ ____ _____ should not perish, but have everlasting life.

22. And this is the condemnation, that light is come into the world, and men loved _____ rather than _____, because their deeds were evil. For every one that doeth evil _____ _____ _____, neither cometh to the light, lest his deeds should be reproved.

But he that doeth truth _____ _____ _____ _____,
that his deeds may be made manifest, that they are wrought in God.

23. John answered and said, a man can receive nothing except it be given him
from heaven.   Ye yourselves bear me witness, that I said, I am not the Christ,
_____ _____ ___ _____ _____ _____
_____.

24. He that believeth on the Son hath everlasting life: and he that believeth not
the Son shall not see life; _____ _____ _____ _____
_____ _____ ____ _____.

25. Now Jacob's well was there, Jesus therefore, being wearied with his journey,
_____ _____ ____ _____ _____ and it was about
the sixth hour. There cometh a woman of Samaria to draw water: Jesus said
unto her, _____ _____ ____ _____.

26. Jesus answered and said unto her: whosoever drinketh of this water _____
_____ _____. But whosoever drinketh of the water that
I shall give him _____ _____ _____; but the
water that I give him shall be in him a well of water _____
_____ _____ _____ _____.

27. The woman saith unto him, Sir, I perceive that thou art _____
_____.

28. God is a Spirit: and they that worship him _____ _____
_____ _____ _____ _____ _____ _____.

29. Jesus saith unto her, I that speak unto thee _____ _____.

30. And said unto the woman now we believe, not because of thy saying: for
we have heard him ourselves, and know that this is indeed the Christ, _____
_____ ____ _____ _____.

31. Then said Jesus unto him, except ye see signs and wonders, ye will _____ _____.

32. The nobleman saith unto him, Sir, come down ere my child die. Jesus saith unto him, ____ _____ _____, _____ _____ _____. And the man _____ the word that Jesus had spoken unto him, and went his way. And as he was now going down, his servants met him, and told him, saying, _____ _____ _____. Then inquired he of them the _____ _____ ____ _____ ____ _____. And they said unto him, yesterday at the _____ _____ the fever left him. So the father knew that it was at the _____ _____, in which Jesus said unto him _____ _____ _____ and himself believed, and his whole house. This is again the _____ _____ that Jesus did, when he was come out of Judaea into Galilee.

33. For an angel went down at a certain season into the pool, and _____ _____ _____: whosoever then first after the troubling of the water stepped in was made whole of whatsoever disease he had. And a certain man was there, which had an infirmity _____ _____ _____ _____. When Jesus saw him lie, and knew that he had been now a long time in that case, he saith unto him, _____ _____ ____ _____ _____? The impotent man answered him, Sir, I have no man, _____ _____ _____ ____ _____, to put me into the pool: but while I am coming, another steppeth down before me. Jesus saith unto him, _____ _____ ____ _____ _____ _____ _____. And immediately the man was made whole, and took up his bed, and walked: and on the same day was _____ _____.

34. Afterward Jesus findeth him in the temple, and said unto him, behold, thou art made whole: _____ _____ _____, _____

____ _____ _____ _____ _____

_____.

35. For the Father judgeth no man, but hath committed _____ _____

_____ _____ _____ _____.

36. Verily, verily, I say unto you he that heareth my word and _____

____ _____ _____ _____ _____ has everlasting

life, and shall not come into condemnation, but is passed from _____

_____ _____.

37. And hath given him authority to execute judgement also, because he is the

_____ ____ _____.

38. Ye sent unto John, and he _____ _____ unto

the truth.

39. For had ye believed Moses ye would have believed me _____ _____

_____ ____ _____.

40. There is a lad here, which hath five barley loaves and two small fishes: but

what are they _____ _____ _____?

41. Therefore they gathered them together and filled twelve baskets with the

fragment of five barley loaves, which remained _____ _____

_____ unto them that had eaten.

42. So when they had rowed about five and twenty or thirty furlong, they

see Jesus _____ ____ _____ _____, and

drawing nigh unto the ship: and they were afraid. But he saith unto them, it

is I, _____ _____ _____.

43. And Jesus said unto them, I am the bread of life: he that cometh to me _
_____ _____ _____; and he that believeth
on me _____ _____ _____.

44. Verily, verily, I say unto you, he that believeth on me hath _____

_____ _____.

45. I am _____ bread of life.

46. Whoso eateth my flesh, and drinketh my blood, hath eternal life and ___
_____ _____ _____ _____ at the last day.

47. It is the spirit that quickened; the flesh profited nothing; the words I speak
unto you, _____ _____ _____, and they are
life.

48. Jesus answered them, have not I chosen you twelve and _____ ____
_____ ____ ___ _____?

49. Jesus answered them, and said, my doctrine is not mine _____ ____
_____ _____ _____.

50. But, lo, he speaketh boldly, and they say nothing unto him. Do the rulers
know indeed that _____ ____ _____ _____
_____?

51. Then cried Jesus in the temple as he taught, saying, ye both know me, and ye
know whence I am ; and I am not come of myself, but he that sent me is true,
whom ye know not. But ___ _____ _____; _____
___ _____ _____ _____, and he hath sent me.

52. In the last day, that great day of the feast, Jesus stood and cried saying, if
any man thirst, let him come unto me, and drink. He that believeth on me, as

the scripture hath said, out of his _____ _____ _____

_____ ____ _____ _____ .

53. So when they continued asking him, he lifted up himself, and said unto them, he that is without sin among you, _____ _____ _____

_____ ___ _____ ___ _____ . And again he stooped down, and wrote on the ground.

54. She said, no man, Lord. And Jesus said unto her, _____

_____ _____ _____ _____ : _____ _____

_____ _____ _____ .

55. Then Jesus spoke again unto them saying, I am the light of the world: he that followed me shall not walk in _____ , but shall have the _____ ____ _____ .

56. Then said they unto him, where is thy Father? Jesus answered, ye neither know me, nor my Father: if ye had known me, ____ _____

_____ _____ _____ _____

_____ .

57. Then said Jesus to those Jews which believed on him, if ye continue in my word, then are ye my disciples indeed.   And ye shall know the truth, _____

_____ _____ _____ _____

_____ _____ .

58. Your father Abraham rejoiced to see my day: _____ _____ _____

_____ , _____ _____ _____ .

59. Jesus said unto them, verily, verily, I say unto you, _____

_____ _____ , ___ _____ .

60. When he had thus spoken, _____ _____ ____ _____
_____, and made clay of the spittle, and he _____
_____ _____ of the blind man with clay.

61. He answered and said, a man that is called Jesus made clay and anointed mine eyes, and said unto me, go to the pool of Siloam, and wash; and I went and washed, _____ ___ _____ _____.

62. But by what means he now seeth, we know not; or who hath opened his eyes, we know not; _____ _____ _____ _____; _____ _____, ____ _____ _____ _____ _____.

63. My sheep hear my voice, and I know them, _____ _____ _____ _____. And I give unto them eternal life; and they shall never perish, neither shall any man _____ _____ _____ ____ ____ _____. My Father, which gave them me, is greater than all and ____ _____ ____ _____ to pluck them out of my Father's hand. I and my Father are _____.

64. If I do not the works of my Father, believe me not. But if I do, though ye believe not me _____ _____ _____: that ye may know, and believe, that the _____ ____ ____ _____, _____ ___ _____ _____.

65. Then said Jesus unto them plainly, Lazarus is dead. And I am glad for your sakes that I was not there, ____ _____ _____ _____ _____ _____; nevertheless let us go into him.

66. Then when Jesus came, he found that he had _____ ____ _____ _____ _____ _____ _____.

67. Martha saith unto him, I know that he shall rise again in the resurrection at the last day. Jesus said unto her, ___ _____ _____ _____,

and the life; he that believeth in me, though he were dead, _____ _____

_____ _____. And whosoever liveth and believeth in me _____

___ _____ _____.

68. When Jesus therefore saw her weeping, and the Jews also weeping which
came with her, _____ _____ ____ _____ _____,

_____ _____ _____.

69. Jesus wept.

70. Then they took away the stone from the place where the dead was laid. And
Jesus lifted up his eyes, and said Father, I thank thee that thou hast heard me.
And I knew that thou hearest me always; _____ _____

____ _____ _____ which stand by I said it, that they may

_____ that thou hast sent me. And when he thus had spoken,
he cried with a loud voice, _____, _____ _____.
And he that was dead came forth, bound hand and foot with graveclothes and
his face was bound about with a napkin. Jesus said unto them, _____

_____, _____ _____ _____ _____.

71. Father, glorify thy name. then came there a voice from heaven, saying, I
have both glorified it and will glorify it again. The people therefore, that stood
by, and heard it, _____ _____ ____ _____:
others said, an angel spake to him. Jesus answered and said, this voice came
not because of me, _____ _____ _____ _____. Now
is the judgement of this world; now shall the prince of this world be cast out.
And I, if I be lifted up from the earth, _____ _____ _____

_____ _____ _____.

72. Now before the feast of the Passover, when Jesus knew that his hour was
come that he should depart out of this world unto the Father, having loved his
own which were in the world, he loved them unto the end. And supper being
ended, _____ _____ having now put into the _____

____ _____ _____, Simon's son, ____ _____

_____.

73. If ye know these things, happy are ye ____ ____ ____ _____.

74. When Jesus had thus said, he was troubled in spirit, and testified, and said, verily, verily, I say unto you, that one of you _____ _____

_____.

75. A new commandment I give unto you, that ye love one another; as I have loved you, _____ ____ _____ _____ _____

_____.

76. Let not your heart be troubled; ye believe in God, _____

_____ _____ _____.

77. Jesus saith unto him, I am the way, the truth and the life; ____ _____

_____ _____ _____ _____, _____

____ _____.

78. And whatsoever ye shall ask in my name, _____ _____ ___

_____, that the Father may be glorified in the Son. If ye shall ask any thing in my name, ___ _____ _____ _____. if ye love me, _____

_____ _____. And I will pray the Father, and he shall give you another _____, that he may abide with you for ever.

79. But the Comforter, which is the _____ _____ whom the Father will send in my name, he shall teach you all things, and _____

_____ _____ ____ _____ _____,

whatsoever I have said unto you.

80. I am the vine, ye are the branches: he that abideth in me and I in him, the same bringeth forth much fruit for without me _____ _____ _____

_____.

81. If ye abide in me, and my words abide in you, ye shall ask what ye will, and

____ _____ ____ _____ _____ _____.

82. These things have I spoken unto you, that my _____ might remain in you, and that your joy _____ ____ _____.

83. And ye all shall bear witness, because ye have been with me _____

_____ _____.

84. Nevertheless I tell you the truth; it is expedient for you that I go away: for if I go not away _____ _____ _____ _____

_____ _____ _____, but if I depart, I will send him unto you.

85. Howbeit when he, the Spirit of Truth, is come, he will guide you into all truth: for he _____ _____ _____ _____ _____
but whatsoever he shall hear, _____ _____ ____ _____
and he will show you things to come.

86. Verily, verily, I say unto you, that ye shall weep and lament, but the world shall rejoice and ye shall be sorrowful, _____ _____ _____

_____ ____ _____ _____ _____.

87. A woman when she is in travail hath sorrow, because her hour is come; but as soon as she is delivered of the child, _____ _____

____ _____ _____ _____ for joy that a man is born into the world.

88. And in that day ye shall ask me nothing. Verily, verily, I say unto you,
_____ ye shall ask the Father ____ _____ _____,
he will give it you.

89. At that day ye shall ask in my name; and I say not unto you, _____
____ _____ _____ the Father for you.

90. For the Father himself loveth you, because ye have loved me, and have
_____ that I came _____ _____ _____.

91. As thou hast given him power over all flesh, that he should give eternal life
to as many as thou hast given him. And this is life eternal, that they might know
thee the _____ _____ _____ _____ _____
_____, whom thou hast sent. I have _____ thee
on the earth; I have _____ _____ _____ which
thou gavest _____ _____ _____.

92. Now they have known that all things whatsoever thou hast given me ___
_____ _____.

93. I pray for them; I pray not for the world, but for them which thou hast given
me; _____ _____ _____ _____.

94. While I was with them in the world, I kept them in thy name; those that
thou gavest me I have kept, _____ _____ _____ _____ ____
_____, but the Son of perdition; that the scripture might be fulfilled.

95. I have given them thy word; and the world hath hated them, _____
_____ _____ _____ _____ _____ _____
even as I am not of the world.

96. Sanctify them through thy truth; _____ _____ _____
_____.

97. And I have declared unto them thy name, and will declare it; that the love wherewith thou hast love me may be in them, _____ ____ _____ _____.

98. Then asked he them again, whom seek ye? And they said, _____ ____ _____. Jesus answered, I have told you that ____ _____ _____; if therefore ye seek me, let these go their way; that the saying might be fulfilled, which he spake, of them which thou gavest me _____ ____ _____ _____.

99. Jesus answered him, I spake openly to the world; I even taught in the synagogue, and in the temple, whither the Jews always resort, _____ ____ _____ _____ ___ _____ _____.

100. Peter then denied again; and _____ the cock crew.

101. Then Pilate entered into the _____ _____ _____, and called Jesus, and said unto him, art thou the _____ ____ _____ _____?

102. Pilate saith unto him, what is truth? And when he had said this, he went out again unto the Jews, and saith unto them, ___ _____ ____ _____ ____ _____ _____ _____.

103. And the soldiers plaited a crown of thorns, and put it on his head, and they put on him ___ _____ _____.

104. Jesus answered, thou couldest have no power at all against me, _____ ____ _____ _____ _____ ___ _____: therefore he that delivered me unto thee hath _____ _____ _____.

105. When Jesus therefore had received the vinegar, he said ____ ____ _____; and he bowed his head, and gave up the ghost.

106. But when they came to Jesus, and saw that he was dead already, _____ _____ _____ _____ _____. But one of the soldiers with a spear pierced his side, and forthwith came there out _____ _____ _____.

107. For these things were done, that the scripture should be fulfilled, ___ _____ ____ _____ _____ _____ ____ _____. And again another scripture saith, they shall look on him whom they pierced.

108. And the napkin, that was about his head, not lying with the linen clothes, but wrapped together ____ ___ _____ ____ _____.

109. But Mary stood without at the sepulchre weeping: and as she wept, she stooped down and looked into the scpulchre, and seeth _____ _____ ____ _____, sitting, the one at the _____, and the other at the _____ where the body of Jesus had lain. And they say unto her, Woman, why weepest thou? She saith unto them, because they have _____ _____ ____ _____, and I know not where they laid him. And when she had thus said she turned herself back, _____ _____ _____ _____, and knew not that it was Jesus.

110. Jesus saith unto her, _____ _____ _____, for I am not yet ascended to my Father; but go to my brethren, and say unto them, ___ _____ _____ _____ _____, and your Father; and to _____ _____ and your God.

111. And when he had so said, he showed unto them _____ _____ _____ _____ _____. Then were the disciples glad, when they saw the Lord.

112. And when he had said this, _____ _____ ____ _____
and saith unto them, receive ye _____ _____ _____.

113. But Thomas, one of the twelve, called Didymus, was not with them when
_____ _____.

114. Jesus saith unto him, _____ because thou hast seen me, thou
hast believed: Blessed are they that have _____ _____, _____
_____ _____ _____.

115. This is now the third time that Jesus showed himself to his disciples, after
that he _____ _____ _____ _____ _____.

116. Peter seeing him saith to Jesus, Lord, and what shall this man do?
Jesus saith unto him, if I will that he tarry till I come, what is that to thee?
_____ _____.

117. And there are also many other things, _____ _____
_____, the which, if they should be written every one, I suppose that even
_____ _____ _____ could not contain _____
_____ _____ _____ ____ _____.

AMEN.

THE END ST. JOHN

ACTS

1. And being assembled together with them, commanded with them, commanded
them that _____ _____ _____ _____ _____
_____, _____ _____ for the promise of the
Father, which, saith he, ye have heard of me. For John truly baptized with water;

but ye shall be baptized _____ _____ _____ _____,
not many days hence.

2. But ye shall receive power, after that the Holy Ghost is come upon you: and ye shall be witness unto me both in _____, and in all _____, and in _____, and unto the uttermost part of the earth! And when he had spoken these things, while they beheld, he was taken up; and a cloud _____ _____ _____ ____ _____ _____. And while they looked steadfastly toward heaven as he went up, behold, two men stood by them in white apparel; which also said, ye men of Galilee, why stand ye gazing up into heaven? This same Jesus, which is taken up from you into heaven, _____ ____ _____ ____ _____ _____ as ye have seen him go into heaven.

3. And they prayed and said, thou, Lord, which knowest the hearts of _____ _____,   show whether of these _____   thou has chosen.

4. And they gave forth their lots; and the lot fell upon _____; and he was numbered with the _____ _____.

5. And when the day of Pentecost was fully come, they were all with _____ _____ ____ _____ _____.

6. And suddenly there came a sound from heaven as of a _____ _____ _____,   and it filled all the house where they were sitting.

7. And they were all filled with the _____ _____, and began to speak with _____ _____, as the Spirit gave them utterance.

8. Others mocking said, these men are full of new _____.

9. And it shall come to pass in the last days, saith God, ____ _____

_____ _____ _____ _____ _____ _____

_____ _____; and your sons and your daughters _____

_____, and your young men shall see _____,

and your old men shall _____ _____.

10. And it shall come to pass, that whosoever shall call on the name of the Lord

_____ ____ _____.

11. Then Peter said unto them, repent and be baptized every one of you in the name of Jesus Christ for the remission of sins, and ye shall receive the _____

____ _____ _____ _____.

12. And with many other words did he testify and exhort, saying, save yourselves from this _____ _____.

13. Then they that gladly received his word were _____; and the same day there were added unto them about _____ _____

_____ _____.

14. And all that believed were together, and had all things _____.

15. And a certain man lame from his mother's womb was carried, whom they laid daily at the gate of the temple which is called _____, to ask alms of them that entered into the temple.

16. Then Peter said, silver and gold have I none; _____ _____ ____

___ _____ _____ ___ _____ in the name of Jesus Christ of Nazareth _____ ____ _____ _____. And he took him by the right hand and lifted him up; and immediately his feet and ankle bones

_____ _____.

17. But ye denied the Holy One and the Just, and desired a murderer to be granted unto you. And killed the Prince of life, who God hath raised from the

Acts

dead whereof we are witness. And his name _____ _____
____ _____ _____ hath made this man strong, whom ye see and know; yea, _____ _____ which is by him hath given him this perfect soundness in the presence of you all.

18. Ye are the children of the prophet, and of the covenant which God made with our fathers, saying, _____ _____, and in thy seed shall all the kindreds of the earth _____ _____.

19. And they laid hands on them, and put them in hold _____ _____ _____ _____;   for it was now eventide.

20. Now when they saw the boldness of Peter and John, and perceived that they were unlearned and ignorant men, they marvelled; and they took knowledge of them, that they had _____ _____ _____ .

21. And they called them and commanded them not to speak at all nor teach _____ _____ _____ _____ _____.

22. So when they had further threatened them, they let them go finding nothing how they might punish them, because of the people _____ _____ ____ _____ _____ for that which was done.

23. And when they heard that, they lifted up their voice _____ _____ _____ _____ _____ and said Lord, thou art God, which hast made _____ _____ _____ _____ _____ _____, and all that in them is.

24. And laid them down at the apostles' feet; and _____ was made unto every man _____ _____ _____ _____ _____.

25. But a certain man named Ananias, with Sapphira, his wife, sold a possession. And _____ _____ _____ of the price, his wife also being privy to it, and brought a certain part, _____ _____ _____ _____ _____ _____'s _____. but Peter said Ananias why hath Satan filled thine heart ____ _____ ____ _____ _____ _____, and to keep back part of the price of the land.

26. And Ananias hearing these words fell down, and _____ _____ _____ _____; and great fear came on all them that heard these things.

27. And it was about the space of three hours after, when his wife, not knowing what was done, _____ _____.

28. Then Peter said unto her, how is it that ye have agreed together to tempt _____ _____ ____ _____ _____? Behold, the feet of them which have buried thy husband _____ ____ _____ _____, and shall carry thee out. Then fell she down straightway at his feet, and _____ ____ _____ _____; and the young men came in, and found her dead, and, carrying her forth _____ _____ ____ _____ _____.

29. Insomuch that they brought forth the sick into the streets, and laid them on beds and couches, that at the least the _____ ____ _____ _____ _____ might overshadow some of them.

30. And laid their hands on the apostles and put them in the common _____. But the angel of the Lord by night _____ _____ _____ _____, and brought them forth and said, go, stand and speak in the temple to the people all the words of this life.

31. Then Peter and the other apostles answered and said, _____ _____ ____ _____ _____ _____ _____ _____.

32. And we are his witness of these things, and so is also _____ _____ _____, whom God hath given to them _____ _____ _____.

33. And daily in the temple, and in every house, they ceased not to teach and preach _____ _____.

34. And Stephen, full of faith and power, did great wonders and miracles _____ _____ _____.

35. And they were not able to resist the _____ _____ _____ _____ by which he spake.

36. And all that sat in the council, looking steadfastly on him, saw his face as it had been _____ _____ ____ ____ _____.

37. And he gave him the Covenant of Circumcision and so _____ _____ _____, and circumcised him the eighth day; and Isaac begat _____ and Jacob begat _____ _____ _____.

38. And the patriarchs, moved with envy, sold Joseph into Egypt; _____ _____ _____ _____ _____.

39. In which time Moses was born, and was exceeding fair, and nourished up in his father's house _____ _____; and when he was cast out, _____'s _____ took him up and nourished him for her _____ _____.

40. And when he was full forty years old, it came into his heart to visit his brethren the _____   _____   _____.

41. Wilt thou kill me, as thou diddest the Egyptian yesterday? Then _____ Moses at this saying, and was a stranger in the land of _____ where he begat _____   _____.   And when forty years were expired, there appeared to in the wilderness of Mount Sina, an angel of the Lord in a _____ ____ _____ ____ ___ _____.   When Moses saw it, he wondered at the sight; and as he drew near to behold it _____ _____ _____ _____ _____ _____ _____ _____, Saying, I am the God of thy fathers, the God of Abraham, and the father of Isaac, and the God of Jacob. Then Moses trembled, and durst not behold. Then said the Lord to him, _____ _____ _____ _____ _____ _____ _____; _____ _____ _____ _____ _____ _____ ____ _____ _____.

42. But he, being full of the Holy Ghost, looked up steadfast into heaven, and saw the glory of God, and _____ _____ ____ _____ _____ _____ ____ _____.

43. And cast him out of the city and _____ _____ and the witness laid down their clothes at a young man's feet, _____ _____ _____ _____.

44. And they stoned Stephen, calling upon God, and saying, Lord Jesus receive my spirit and he kneeled down, and cried with a loud voice, _____ ___ _____ _____ _____ ____ _____ _____. And when he had said this, he fell asleep.

45. And Saul was consenting unto his death. And at that time there was ___ _____ _____ _____ _____ _____ which was at Jerusalem; and they were all scattered abroad

throughout the regions of _____ _____ _____
except the apostles.

46. As for Saul, he made havoc of the church, entering into every house,

_____ _____ _____ _____ _____
committed them to prison.

47. But there was a certain man, called Simon, which beforetime in the same
city used sorcery and bewitched the people of Samaria, giving out that himself
was some _____ _____.

48. And when Simon saw that through laying on of the apostles' hands the Holy
Ghost was given, he _____ _____ _____.

49. But Peter said unto him, thy money _____ with thee, because
thou hast thought that the _____ ____ _____ may be
purchased with money.

50. Repent therefore of this thy wickedness, and pray God, if perhaps the
_____ ____ _____ _____ may be
forgiven thee.

51. Then the Spirit said, unto Phillip, go near, and   join thyself to this
_____.

52. And Phillip said, if thou believest with all thine heart thou mayest. And he
answered and said, ____ _____ _____ _____
_____ ____ _____ _____ ____ _____.
And he commanded the chariot to _____ _____; and
they went down, both into the water, both Philip and the eunuch; and he
_____ _____. And when they were come up out of the water,

_____ _____ ____ _____ _____ _____

_____ _____, that the eunuch saw him no more; and he went on his way rejoicing.

53. And as he journeyed, he came near Damascus and suddenly there shined round about him ___ _____ _____ _____. And he fell to the earth, and heard a voice saying unto him Saul, _____, _____ _____ ____?

54. And he was three days _____ _____, and neither did eat nor drink.

55. And there was a certain disciple at _____ _____ _____, and to him said the Lord in a vision, Ananias. And he said, behold, ___ ____ _____, _____.

56. But the Lord said unto him, go thy way; _____ ____ ____ ___ _____ _____ _____ _____, to bear my name before the Gentiles, and kings and the children of Israel.

57. And immediately there fell from his eyes as it had been _____; and he received _____ forthwith, and arose, and was _____.

58. And straightway he preached Christ in the synagogues, that he is the _____ ____ _____.

59. And after that many days were fulfilled, the Jews took _____ ____ _____ _____.

60. Then the disciples took him by night, and let him down by the _____ _____ ___ _____.

61. But barnabus took him, and brought him to the apostles, and declared unto them how he had seen the Lord in the way and that he had spoken to him and

Acts

how he had _____ _____ at Damascus in the

_____ ____ _____.

62. But Peter put them all forth, and kneeled down, and prayed; and turning him to the body said Tabitha, arise. And she opened her eyes; and when she saw Peter, _____ _____ _____.

63. He saw in a vision evidently about the nineth hour of the day _____ _____ ____ _____ _____ ____ ____ _____, and saying unto him, Cornelius, and when he looked on him, he was afraid, and said, what is it Lord? And he said unto him, _____ _____ _____ _____ _____ _____ _____ ____ _____ ___ _____ _____ _____.

64. And when he had declared all these things unto them, he sent _____ _____ _____.

65. And he became very hungry, and would have eaten; but while they made ready, ____ _____ _____ ___ _____.

66. And the voice spake unto him again the second time, what God hath cleansed, _____ _____ _____ _____ _____.

67. While Peter thought on the vision, the Spirit said unto him, behold, three men seek thee. Arise therefore, and get thee down, and go with them _____ _____; _____ _____ _____ _____ _____.

68. But Peter took him up, saying, stand up; ___ _____ _____ ____ ___ _____.

69. But in every nation he that feareth him and worketh righteousness is accepted _____ _____.

164

70.   To him give all the prophets witness, that through his name whosoever believeth in him _____ _____ _____ _____ _____. While Peter yet spake these words, _____ _____ _____ fell on all them which heard the word.

71.   Can any man forbid water, that these should not be baptized, which have received _____ _____ _____ ____ _____ _____ _____?

72.   And as I began to speak, the Holy Ghost fell on them, as on us at the beginning. Then remembered I the word of the Lord, how that he said, John indeed baptized with water, but ye shall be baptized with the Holy Ghost. Forasmuch then as God gave them the like gift as he did unto us, _____ _____ _____ _____ _____ _____ _____; what was I, that I could withstand God?   When they heard these things, they held their peace, and glorified God saying, _____ _____ _____ _____ ____ _____ _____ _____ _____ _____ _____.

Now they which were scattered abroad upon the persecution that arose about _____ traveled as far as Phenice, and Cyprus, and Antioch _____ _____ _____ ____ _____ _____ _____ _____ _____ _____.

73.   And he killed James the brother of John with the _____.

74.   Peter therefore was kept in prison: but prayers was made _____ _____ _____ of the church unto _____ _____ _____.

75.   And when Herod would have brought him forth, the same night _____ _____ _____ between two soldiers, bound with two chains: and the keepers before the door kept the prison.

76. And , behold, the angel of the Lord came upon him and a light shined in the prison; and he smote Peter on the side and raised him up saying, _____ _____ _____. _____ _____ _____ _____ _____ _____ _____ _____.

77. And when Peter was come to himself, he said, now I know of a surety, that the Lord hath _____ _____ _____, And hath delivered me out of the hand of Herod, and from all the _____ of the people of the Jews.

78. And upon a set day Herod arrayed in royal apparel, sat upon his throne, and made an oration unto them. And the people gave a shout, saying, it is the voice of a god, and not of a man. And immediately _____ _____ _____ _____ _____ smote him, because he gave not God the glory; _____ _____ _____ _____ _____ _____ _____ gave up the ghost.

79. And when they had gone through the isle unto Paphos, they found a certain sorcerer, _____ _____ _____, a Jew, whose name as _____ - _____.

80. Then Saul, (who also is called Paul) filled with the Holy Ghost, _____ _____ _____ ____ _____.

81. And now, behold, the hand of the Lord is upon thee, and thou shalt be blind, _____ _____ _____ _____ _____ _____ _____. And immediately there fell on him ___ _____ _____ ___ _____ and he went about seeking some to _____ _____ ____ _____ _____.

82. Then Paul stood up, and beckoning with his hands said, men of Israel, and ye that fear God, _____ _____.

83. And when he had removed him, he raised up unto them David to be their king; to whom also he gave testimony, and said, I have found David, the son of Jesse, a man after mine own heart, _____   _____

_____   _____   _____   _____.

84. And as John fulfilled his course, he said, whom think ye that I am? I am not he. But behold, there cometh one after me, _____   _____

_____   _____   _____   ___   ____   _____   _____

_____   _____.

85. And by him all that believe are justified from all things, from which ye could not be justified _____   _____   _____   _____

_____.

86. And the next Sabbath day came almost the whole city together to hear the word of _____. But when the Jews saw the multitudes, they were filled with _____, and spake against those things which were spoken by _____ contradicting and blaspheming.

87. But they shook off the dust of their feet _____   _____, and came unto Iconium.

88. But the unbelieving Jews stirred up the Gentiles, and _____   _____ _____   _____ affected against the brethren.

89. They were ware of it, and fled unto Lystra and Derbe, cities of Lycaonia, and unto the region that lieth round about; and there they _____ _____   _____. And there sat a certain man at Lystra, impotent in his feet, being a cripple from his mother's womb, _____   _____ _____   _____. The same heard Paul speak; who steadfastly beholding him, and preceiving that he had _____   ____   ____ _____, said in a loud voice, stand upright on thy feet. _____

____   _____   _____   _____.

90. And there came thither certain Jews from Antioch and Iconium, who persuaded the people, and , having _____ _____, drew him out of the city, _____ _____ _____ _____ _____.

91. And when they had ordained them elders in every church, and had prayed with fasting, they _____ _____ ____ _____ _____,   on whom they believe.

92. And God, which knoweth the hearts, bare them witness, giving them the Holy Ghost, even as he did unto us. And put no difference between us and them, _____ _____ _____ ____ _____.

93. And they wrote letters by them after this manner; _____ _____ _____ _____ _____ _____ _____ _____ unto the brethren which are of the Gentiles in Antioch and Syria and Cilicia.

94. For it seemed good to the Holy Ghost, and to us, to lay upon you ____ _____ _____ _____ _____ _____ _____. That ye abstain from meats offered to idols, and from blood, and from things strangled, and from fornication; from which if ye keep yourselves, ye shall do well. Fare ye well.

95. And the contention was so sharp between them that _____ _____ _____ _____ _____ _____ _____; and so Barnabus took Mark, and sailed unto Cyprus. And Paul chose _____ _____ _____, being recommend by the brethren unto the grace of God.

96. The same followed Paul and us, and cried, saying, these men are the servants of the most High God, which show unto us the way of salvation. And this did she many days. _____ _____, _____ _____,

_____ _____ _____ ____ _____ _____,
I command thee in the name of Jesus Christ to come out of her. And he came out the same hour.

97. And when they had laid many stripes upon them, _____ _____
_____ _____ _____, charging the jailer to keep them safety.

98. And at midnight Paul and Silas prayed and sang praises unto God _____
_____ _____ _____ _____.

99. But Paul cried with a loud voice, saying, do thyself no harm; _____
_____ _____ _____ _____.

100. And they came and besought them, and brought them out, and desired them to depart _____ ____ _____ _____.

101. And then immediately the brethren sent away Paul to go as it were to the sea; _____ _____ _____ _____
_____ _____ _____.

102. Now while Paul waited for them at Athens, his spirit was stirred in him, when he saw the city _____ _____ _____
_____.

103. For as I passed by, and beheld your devotions, I found an altar with this inscription, ____ _____ _____ _____. Whom therefore ye ignorantly worship, him declare I unto you. God that made the world and _____ _____ _____, seeing that he is Lord of heaven and earth, dwelleth _____ _____ temples made with hands.

104. For in him we live, and move, and have our being; as certain also of your own poets have said, _____ _____ _____ _____

_____.

105. And the times of this ignorance God winked at; but now commandeth

_____ _____ _____ _____ ____ _____.

106. So Paul _____ from among them.

107. Then spake the Lord to Paul in the night ____ ____ _____,

be not afraid, but speak, and _____ _____ _____ _____;

for I am with thee, and no man shall set on thee to hurt thee; for I have much

people in this city.

108. And Paul after this tarried there yet a good while, and then took his leave of

the brethren, and sailed thence into Syria and with him _____

_____ _____ having shorn his head in Cenchrea, _____

_____ _____ ___ _____.

109. And he began to speak boldly in the synagogue; whom when Aquila

and Priscilla had heard, _____ _____ _____ _____

_____ , and expounded unto him the way of _____ _____

_____.

110. Then said Paul, John verily baptized with the baptism of repentance, saying

unto the people, that they should believe on him which should _____

_____ _____ , that is, on Jesus Christ. When they heard this, they

were baptized ____ _____ _____ ____ _____ _____

and when Paul had laid his hands upon them, _____ _____ _____

_____ _____ _____; and they spake with tongues, and

prophesied. And all the men were about _____.

111. And the evil spirit answered and said, Jesus I know, and Paul I know;

_____ _____ _____ ____? And the man in whom the evil spirit was leaped on them and overcame them, and prevailed against them, so that they fled out of that house _____ _____ _____.

112. And many that believed came, and confessed, and showed _____ _____.

113. Some therefore, cried one thing, and some another: for the _____ _____ _____; and the more part knew not wherefore they were come together.

114. For we are in danger to be called in question for this day's uproar. There being no cause whereby we may give an account of this concourse. And when he had thus spoken, _____ _____ _____ _____.

115. And there sat in a window a certain young man named Eutychus, being fallen into a deep sleep; and as Paul was long preaching, he sunk down with sleep and _____ _____ _____ _____ _____ _____ and was taken up dead. And Paul went down, and fell on him, and embracing him said, trouble not yourselves ; _____ _____ _____ ____ ____ _____.

116. And now, behold, I know that ye all among whom I have gone preaching the kingdom of God _____ _____ ____ _____ ____ _____ wherefore, I take you to record this day that I am pure from the _____ ____ _____ _____. For I have not shunned to declare unto you all the counsel of God. Take heed therefore unto yourselves, and to all the flock, over the which _____ _____ _____ _____ _____ _____ _____, to feed the church of God, which he hath purchased _____ _____ _____ _____.

117. I have shown you all things, how that so labouring ye ought to support the weak, and remember the words of the Lord Jesus, how he said, it is more

_____ ____ _____ _____ _____

_____.

118. And when he had thus spoken he kneeled down and prayed with them all. And they all wept sore, and _____ ____ _____'s _____ and kissed him. Sorrowing most of all for the words which he spake that they should see his face ____ _____. And they accompanied him unto the ship.

119. And finding disciples, we tarried there seven days: who said to Paul through the spirit, that he _____ _____ go up to Jerusalem.

120. Then Paul answered, What mean ye to weep and to break mine heart? For I am ready not to be bound only, but also _____ _____ _____ _____ for the name of the Lord Jesus.

121. And when the seven days were almost ended, the Jews which were Asia, when they saw him ____ _____ _____, stirred up all the people, and _____ _____ ____ _____.

122. And as they went about to kill him, tidings came unto the chief captain of the band, that _____ _____ _____ ____ ____ _____.

123. And when he had given him license, Paul stood on the stairs and beckoned with the hand unto the people. And when there was made a great silence, ____ _____ _____ _____ ____ _____ _____ _____ saying, men, brethren, and fathers, hear ye _____ _____ which I make now unto you.

124. I am verily a man which am a Jew, born in Tarsus, a city in Cilicia, yet brought up in this city at the feet of Gamaliel, and _____

_____ to the perfect manner of the _____ ____

_____ _____, and was zealous toward God, as ye all are

this day.

125. And I answered, who art thou Lord? And he said unto me, I am Jesus of

Nazareth, _____ _____ _____.

126. And I said, What shall I do Lord? And the Lord said unto me, arise, and

go into Damascus; and there it shall be told thee of _____ _____

_____ _____ _____ _____ _____

____ ____.

127. Came unto me, and stood, and said unto me Brother Saul, receive thy

sight and the _____ _____ __ ___ _____ _____

_____ _____.

128. And now why tarriest thou? Arise, and be baptized, and _____

_____ _____ _____, calling on the name of the Lord.

129. And when the blood of thy martyr _____ _____

_____, ___ _____ _____ _____

_____, and consenting unto his death and kept the raiment of them that slew

him.

130. And when he had so said, there arose a dissension between the Pharisees

and the Sadducees: _____ _____ _____ _____

_____.

131. And there arose a great cry; and the scribes that were of the Pharisees' part

arose, and strove saying, _____ _____ ____ _____ ____

_____ _____: but if a spirit or an angel hath spoken to him, _____

____ _____ _____ _____ _____.

132. So the chief captain then let the young man depart, _____ _____

_____, see thou tell no man that thou hast shown hast shown _____

_____ _____ _____.

133. But this I confess unto thee, that after the way which they call heresy, so
worship I the God of my fathers, believing all things which are written in the
law and in the prophets; and have hope toward God, which they themselves also
allow, that _____ _____ _____ ___ _____

_____ _____ _____, _____ _____ _____ _____

_____ _____. And herein do I exercise myself, to have always

a conscience _____ _____ _____ toward God and

toward men.

134. And as he reasoned of righteousness , temperance, and judgement to
come, Felix trembled. And answered, _____ _____ _____ _____

_____ _____; when I have a convenience season, ____ _____

_____ _____ _____.

135. Then said Paul, I stand at Caesar's judgement seat, where I ought to be
judged: _____ _____ _____ _____ ____ _____

_____ _____ as thou very well knowest.

136. Then Festur, when he had conferred with the council, answered, Hast thou
appealed unto Caesar? _____ _____ _____

_____ _____.

137. But when I found that he had committed nothing worthy of death, and that
he himself hath appealed to Augustus, ____ _____ _____

_____ _____ _____.

138. For it seemeth to me unreasonable _____ _____ _____

_____ and not withal to signify the crimes laid against him.

139. At midday, O king, I saw in the way ___ _____ _____

_____ _____ _____ _____

_____ _____ _____ shinning round about me and them which

journeyed with me.

140. But rise, and stand upon thy feet; for I have appeared unto thee f or this

purpose, ____ _____ _____ ___ _____

_____ ___ _____ both of these things which thou hast

seen, and of those things in the which I will appear unto thee.

141. To open their eyes, and turn them from _____ _____

_____ and from the power of Satan unto God, that they may

receive forgiveness of sins, and inheritance among them which are sanctified

_____ _____ _____ _____ _____ _____.

142. The Agrippa said unto Paul, almost thou persuades _____ _____

_____ ___ _____.

143. And when they were gone aside, they talked between themselves,

saying, this man doeth _____ _____ _____

_____ _____ _____ _____.

144. And said unto them, sirs, I perceive that this voyage _____ _____

_____ _____ _____ _____ _____.

145. But not long after there arose against it a tempestuous wind called

_____.

146. But after long abstinence Paul stood forth in the midst of them, and said,

sirs, ye should have _____ _____ _____ , and not

have loosed from crete, and to have gained this harm and loss.

147. And the rest, some on boards, and some on broken pieces of the ship. And so it came to pass, that they _____ _____ _____ _____ _____.

148. And when Paul had gathered a bundle of sticks, and laid them on the fire, there came a _____ out of the heat and fastened on his hand.

149. And he shook off the beast into the fire, and felt _____ _____.

150. Who, when they had examined me, would have let me go, because there was _____ _____ _____ _____ _____ _____.

151. And some believed the things which were spoken, _____ _____ _____ _____.

152. And Paul dwelt two whole years in his own hired house,   and received all that came in unto him. _____ _____ _____ _____ _____, _____ _____ _____ _____ _____ _____ the Lord Jesus Christ, with all confidence, no man forbidding him.

THE END THE ACTS

THE OLD TESTAMENT ANSWERS

1. Genesis 1: 1
Answer - God

2. Genesis 1:2
Answer - And the spirit of God moved upon the face of the waters.

3. Genesis 1:5
Answer - a. day   b. night   c. first day

4. Genesis **1:8**
Answer - a. heaven   b. second day

5. Genesis 1:14
Answer - and let them be for signs, and for seasons and for days and years.

6. Genesis 1:27
Answer - a. God   b. Male and female created he him.

7. Genesis 2:2-3
Answer - blessed the seventh day, and sanctified it

8. Genesis 2:7
Answer - Breathed into his nostrils the breath of life and man became a living soul.

9. Genesis - 2: 21-25
Answer - a. and he took one of his ribs   b. which the Lord God had taken from man, made he a woman   c. this is now bone of my bones and flesh of my flesh   d. and they shall be one flesh   e. were not ashamed

10. Genesis 3:4
Answer - a. Not

11. Genesis 3:14
Answer - a. thou art cursed   b. upon thy belly shall thou go, and dust shall thou eat all the days of thy life

12. Genesis 3:21
 Answer - a. and clothed them

13. - Genesis 4:1-2
Answer - a. and she conceived and bare Cain   b. Abel   c. keeper of sheep   d. tiller of the ground

14. Genesis 4:8
Answer - a. that Cain rose up against Abel his brother, and slew him

15. Genesis 4: 13
Answer - a. my punishment is greater than I can bear

16. Genesis 4: 17
Answer - a. and bare Enoch   b. after the name of his son Enoch

17. Genesis 5:3
Answer - a. and called his name Seth

18. Genesis 5:28-29
Answer - a. begat a son   b. Noah   c. because of the ground which the Lord hath cursed

19. Genesis 5:32
Answer - a. Shem, Ham, and Japheth

20. Genesis 6:2
Answer - a. and they took them wives of all which they chose

21. Genesis 6:5
Answer - a. the wickedness of man was great in the earth   b. only evil continually

22. Genesis 6:8
Answer - a. grace in the eyes of the Lord

23. Genesis 6:13
Answer - a. the end of all flesh is come before me   b. I will destroy them with the earth

24. Genesis 6:17
Answer - a. bring a flood of waters upon the earth   b. and every thing that is in the earth shall die

25. Genesis 6:18
Answer - a. and thou shall come into the ark

26. Genesis 6:22
Answer - a. so did he

27. Genesis 7:11-12
Answer - a. in the second month, the seventeenth day of the month   b. windows of heaven were opened   c. forty days and forty nights

28. Genesis 7:24
Answer - a. hundred and fifty days

29. Genesis 8:11
Answer - a. so Noah knew that the waters were abated from off the earth

30. Genesis 8:21
Answer - a. I will not again curse the ground any more for man's sake   b. from his youth   c. as I have done

31. Genesis 9:11-12
Answer - a. a flood to destroy the earth   b. this is the token of the covenant which I make between me and you

32. Genesis 9:13
Answer - a. my bow in the cloud   b. token of a covenant between me and the earth

33. Genesis 9:21
Answer - a. and was drunken

34. Genesis 9:29
Answer - a. Noah   b. and he died

35. Genesis 10:1
Answer - a. Shem, Ham, and Japheth

36. Genesis 11:1
Answer - a. one language, and of one speech

37. Genesis 11:7
Answer - a. not understand one another's speech

38. Genesis 11:26
Answer - a. Abram, Nahor and Haran

39. Genesis 11:28
Answer - a. died before his father Terah

40. Genesis 11:29
Answer - a. the name of Abram's wife was Sarai   b. Nahor's wife, Milcah

41. Genesis 11:30
Answer - a. was barren

42. Genesis 12:1-4
Answer - a. get thee out of thy country and from thy kindred, and from thy father's house   b. and I will bless thee, and make thou name great; and thou shall be a blessing   c. and in thee shall all families of the earth be blessed   d. as the Lord had spoken unto him

43. Genesis 12:12-13
Answer - a. and they will kill me,   b. thou art my sister   c. and my soul shall live because of thee

44. Genesis 12:20
Answer - a. and they sent him away and his wife, and all that he had

45. Genesis 13-2
Answer - a. very

46. Genesis 13:8-9
Answer - a. Let there be no strife I pray thee, between me and thee   b. for we be brethren   c. if thou wilt take the left hand, then I will go to the right

47. Genesis 13-11-12
Answer - a. all the plain of Jordan   b. the land of Canaan

48. Genesis 13: 15-16
Answer - a. I will make thy seed as the dust of the earth

49. Genesis 14:12
Answer - who dwelt in Sodom

50. Genesis 14:16
Answer - a. and also brought again his brother Lot

51. Genesis 15:3
Answer - a. to me thou hast given no seed

52. Genesis 16:2
Answer - a. the Lord hath restrained me from bearing

53. Genesis 16:4
Answer - a. and she conceived   b. her mistress was despised in her eyes

54. Genesis 16: 7
Answer - a. by a fountain of water

55. Genesis 16:10-11
Answer - a. I will multiply thou seed exceedingly   b. numbered   c. Ishmael

56. Genesis 16:15
Answer - a. which Hagar bare, Ishmael

57. Genesis 17:5
Answer - a. Abram   b. Abraham

58. Genesis 17:10-11
Answer - a. every man child among you shall be circumcised   b. a token of the covenant betwixt me and you

59. Genesis 17:15
Answer - a. as for Sarai   b. but Sarah shall be her name

60. Genesis 17:19-20
Answer - a. bear thee a son indeed and thou shalt call his name Isaac   b. Ishmael   c. behold, I have blessed him   d. twelve princes shall he beget

61. Genesis 17:27
Answer - a. were circumcised with him

62. Genesis 18:23
Answer - a. the righteous with the wicked?

63. Genesis 18:26
Answer - a. in Sodom fifty righteous within the city   b. all the place for their sakes

64. Genesis 19:17
Answer - a. look not behind thee   b. thou be consumed

65. Genesis 19:24
Answer - a. upon Sodom and upon Gomorah brimstone and fire

66. Genesis 19:26
Answer - a. looked back   b. became a pillar of salt

67. Genesis 19:31
Answer - a. our father is old   b. to come in unto us

68. Genesis 19:36-38
Answer - a. daughters of Lot with child by their father   b. Moab   c. Moabits   d. Ben-Ammi   e. Ammon unto this day

69. Genesis 20:12
Answer - a. she is the daughter of my father, but not the daughter of my mother

70. Genesis 21:2-3
Answer - a. whom Sarah bare to him Isaac

71. Genesis 21: 14
 Answer - a. and took bread, and a bottle of water   b. Hagar   c. Beer-Sheba

72. Genesis 21:18
Answer - a. for I will make him a great nation

73. Genesis 21:25
Answer - a. because of a well of water

74. Genesis 21:27
Answer - a. and both of them made a covenant

75. Genesis 21:30
Answer - a. thou shall take my hand   b. witness unto me

76. Genesis 22:10
Answer - a. to slay his son

77. Genesis 22:13
Answer - a. behind him a ram caught in the thicket by his horns   b. in the stead of his son

78. Genesis 22:17-18
Answer - a. stars of the heaven, and as the sand which is upon the sea shore   b. because thou hast obeyed my voice

79. Genesis 23:1
Answer - a. the life of Sarah

80. Genesis 23:15
Answer - a. the land is worth four hundred shekels of silver

81. Genesis 23:19
Answer - a. field of Machpelah before Mamre

82. Genesis 23:20
Answer - a. unto Abraham   b. by the sons of Heth

83. Genesis 24:4
Answer - a. take a wife unto my son Isaac

84. Genesis 24: 15
Answer - a. Rebekah came out   b. with a pitcher upon her shoulder

85. Genesis 24:51
Answer - a. take her and go

86. Genesis 25:1-2
Answer a. and her name was Keturah   b. Zimran   c. Jokshan   d. Medan   e. Midian   f. Ishbak   g. Shuah

87. Genesis 25:5
Answer a. he had unto Isaac

88. Genesis 25:7
Answer - a. an hundred threescore and fifteen years

89. Genesis 25:9
Answer - a. Isaac and Ishmael   b. which is before Mamre

90. Genesis 25:10
Answer - a. there was Abraham buried and Sarah his wife

91. Genesis 25:23-27
Answer - a. two nations are in thy womb   b. and the elder shall serve the younger   c. twins in her womb
d. come out red all over like a hairy garment   e. Esau   f. his hand took hold of Esau's heel   g. Jacob   h.
Esau   I. Jacob

92. Genesis 25:28
Answer - a. but Rebekah loved Jacob

93. Genesis 25:33
Answer - a. he sold his birthrights unto Jacob

94. Genesis 26:5
Answer - a. my commandments, my statutes, and my laws

95. Genesis 26:18
Answer - a. for the Philistines had stopped them after the death of Abraham

96. Genesis 26:24
Answer - a. I AM the God of Abraham thy father; fear not for I AM with thee, and will bless thee,

97. Genesis 26:31
Answer - a. sware one to another   b. departed from him in peace

98. Genesis 27:1
Answer - a. he called Esau his eldest son

99. Genesis 27:4
Answer - a. that my soul may bless thee before I die

100. Genesis 27:11
Answer - a. is a hairy man, and I am a smooth man

101. Genesis 27:16
Answer - a. upon his hands, and upon the smooth of his neck

102. Genesis 27:22-24
Answer - a. the voice is Jacob's voice, but the hands are the hands of Esau   b. so he blessed him   c. I AM

103. Genesis 27:30
Answer - a. that Esau his brother came in from his hunting

104. Genesis 27:35
Answer - a. and hath taken away thy blessing

105. Genesis 27:36
Answer - a. he took away my birthright, and behold, now he hast taken away my blessing

106. Genesis 27:41
Answer - a. then will I slay my brother Jacob

107. Genesis - a. 28:12
Answer - a. And the top of it reached to heaven

108. Genesis 28:22
Answer - a. God's house   b. thou shalt give me I will surely give the tenth unto thee

109. Genesis 29:6
Answer - a. behold, Rachel his daughter cometh

110. Genesis 29:16
Answer - a. elder was Leah   b. younger was Rachel

111. Genesis 29:18
Answer - a. I will serve thee seven years for Rachel

112. Genesis 29:23
Answer - a. that he took Leah   b. and he went in unto her

113. Genesis 29:28
Answer - a. and he gave him Rachel his daughter to wife also

114. Genesis 29:32
Answer - a. Reuben   b. looked upon my affliction

115. Genesis 30:9
Answer - a. she took Zilpah her maid, and gave her Jacob to wife

116. Genesis 30:25
Answer - a. Rachel had born Joseph   b. mine own place

117. Genesis 30:39
Answer - a. the rod   b. ringstraked, speckled and spotted

118. Genesis 30:43
Answer - a. increase exceedingly

119. Genesis 31:3
Answer - a. and I will be with thee

120. Genesis 31:11-13
Answer - a. Jacob   b. rams which leap upon the cattle are ringstrake, speckled and grisled   c. Laban   d. the God of Beth-el   e. vowedst a vow unto me

121. Genesis 31:20
Answer - a. unawares to Laban the Syrian

122. Genesis 31:24
Answer - a. take heed that thou speak not to Jacob either good or bad

123. Genesis 31:31
Answer - a. because I was afraid   b. take by force thy daughters from me

124. Genesis 31:41
Answer - a. I served thee fourteen years for thy two daughters

125. Genesis 31:44
Answer - a. make a covenant, I and thou

126. Genesis 31:49
Answer - a. when we are absent, one from another

127. Genesis 31:52
Answer - a. will not pass over this heap to thee   b. shalt not pass over this heap   c. for harm

128. Genesis 32:3
Answer - a. to Esau his brother

129. Genesis 32:8
Answer - a. the other company which is left shall escape

130. Genesis 32:24
Answer - a. wrestled a man with him until the breaking of the day

131. Genesis 32:26
Answer - a. I will not let thee go, except thou bless me

132. Genesis 32:28
Answer - a. but Israel

133. Genesis 32:30
Answer - a. for I have seen God face to face

134. Genesis 33:4
Answer - a. ran to meet him   b. and they wept

135. Genesis 34:15
Answer - a. that every male of you be circumcised

136. Genesis 34:25
Answer - a. Simeon and Levi   b. and came upon the city boldly and slew all the males

137. Genesis 35:1
Answer - a. when thou fleddest from the face of Esau thy brother

138. Genesis 35:10-11
Answer - a. but Israel shall be thy name   b. a nation and a company of nations

139. Genesis 35:13
Answer - a. where he talked with him

140. Genesis 35:18
Answer - a. but his father called him Benjamin

141. Genesis 35:20
Answer - a. that is the pillar of Rachel's grave

142. Genesis 35:22
Answer - a. father's concubine   b. now the sons of Jacob were twelve

143. Genesis 35:23
Answer - a. Reuben   b. Simeon   c. Levi   d. Judah e. Issachar   f. Zebulum

144. Genesis 35:24
Answer - a. Joseph   b. Benjamin

145. Genesis 35:25
Answer - a. Dan   b. Naphtali

146. Genesis 35:26
Answer - a. Gad   b. Asher

147 Genesis 35:28-29
Answer - a. Isaac gave up the ghost and died   b. Esau and Jacob buried him

148. Genesis 36:1
Answer - a. who is Edom

149. Genesis 36:40
Answer - a. Timnah, Alvan, Jetheth

150. Genesis 37:3
Answer - a. more than all his children   b. and he made him a coat of many colours

151. Genesis 37:5
Answer - a. and they hated him yet the more

152. Genesis 37:19
Answer - a. behold, this dreamer cometh

153. Genesis 37:21
Answer - a. let us not kill him

154. Genesis 37:23-24
Answer - a. his coat of many colours   b. and the pit was empty,

155. Genesis 37:28
Answer - a. And sold Joseph to the Ishmeelites for twenty pieces of silver   b. Egypt

156. Genesis 37:34
Answer - a. and mourned for his son many days

157. Genesis 38:26
Answer - a. she had been more righteous than thou

158. Genesis 38:27
Answer - a. behold, twins were in her womb

159. Genesis 39:4
Answer - a. he made him overseer over his house

160. Genesis 39:7
Answer - a. wife cast her eyes upon Joseph   b. lie with me

161. Genesis 39:9
Answer - a. how then can I do this great wickedness, and sin against God?

162. Genesis 39:12
Answer - a. lie with me

163. Genesis 39:19-21
Answer - a. words of his wife   b. that his wrath was kindled   d. and put him into the prison   e. and gave him favour in the sight of the keeper of the prison

164. Genesis 40:5
Answer - a. each man his dream in one night   b. the butler and the baker

165. Genesis 40:12-13
Answer - a. the three branches are three days   b. and restore thee unto thy place

166. Genesis 40:18-19
Answer - a. the three baskets are three days   b. and shall hang thee on a tree

167. Genesis 40:21-23
Answer - a. unto his butlership again   b. hanged the chief baker   c. chief butler   d. but forgot him

168. Genesis 41:25-26
Answer - a. one   b. seven good kine   c. seven years   e. seven good ears   f. seven years; the dream is one

169. Genesis 41:47
Answer - a. the earth brought forth by handfuls

170. Genesis 41:53-54
Answer - a. were ended   b. according as Joseph had said   c. but in all the land of Egypt there was bread

171. Genesis 41:57
Answer - a. Joseph for to buy corn

172. Genesis 42:1
Answer - a. why do ye look one upon another?

173. Genesis 42:3
Answer - a. ten brethren

174. Genesis 42:7
Answer - a. and he knew them   b. from the land of Canaan

175. Genesis 42:15
Answer - a. proved   b. except your youngest brother come hither

176. Genesis 42:23
Answer - a. for he spake unto them by an interpreter

177. Genesis 42:31
Answer - a. we are no spies

178. Genesis 42:32
Answer - a. one is not   b. in the land of Canaan

179. Genesis 43:15
Answer - a. present   b. double money   c. Benjamin

180. Genesis 43:16
Answer - a. bring these men home, and slay, and make ready; for these men shall dine with me at noon

181. Genesis 43:30
Answer - a. and he entered into his chambers, and wept there

182. Genesis 44:28
Answer - a. and I saw him not since

183. Genesis 45:4
Answer - a. come near to me   b. I am Joseph your brother, whom ye sold into Egypt

184. Genesis 45:27-28
Answer - a. the spirit of Jacob their father revived   b. I will go and see him before I die

185. Genesis 46:5
Answer - a. and the sons of Israel carried Jacob their father,

186. Genesis 46:29-30
Answer - a. Israel his father   b. and he fell on his neck and wept on his neck a good while   c. now let me die, since I have seen thy face

187. Genesis 47:20
Answer - a. land of Egypt for Pharaoh   b. so the land became Pharaoh's

188. Genesis 47:28
Answer - a. seventeen years

189. Genesis 47:30
Answer - a. and thou shall carry me out of Egypt and bury me in their buryingplace

190. Genesis 48:19
Answer - a. I know it my son, I know it   b. but truly his younger brother shall be greater than he   c. a multitude of nations

191. Genesis 49:1-2
Answer - a. gather yourselves together   b. and hear, ye sons of Jacob and hearken unto Israel your father

192. Genesis 49:28
Answer - a. twelve tribes of Israel   b. every one according to his blessing, he blessed them

193. Genesis 49:29-33
Answer - a. bury me with my father in the cave that is in the field of Ephron the Hittite   b. field of Machpelah   c. in the land of Canaan   d. Abraham   e. of a burying- place   f. Abraham   g. Sarah   h. Isaac   I. Rebehak   j. Leah   k. from the children of Heth   L. yielded up the ghost, and was gathered unto his people

194. Genesis 50:1-2
Answer - a. wept upon him and kiss him   b. embalm his father; and the physicians embalmed Israel

195. Genesis 50:6
Answer - a. according as he made thee swear

196. Genesis 50:9
Answer - a. and it was a very great company

197. Genesis 50:12-13
Answer - a. into the land of Canaan and buried him   b. Abraham   c. Mamre

198. Genesis 50:17
Answer - a. the trespass of thy brethren, and their sins   b. and Joseph wept when they spake unto him

199. Genesis 50:20
Answer - a. but God meant it unto good

200. Genesis 50:24
Answer - a. to Abraham, to Isaac and to Jacob

201. Genesis 50:25-26
Answer - a. the children of Israel   b. and ye shall carry up my bones from hence   c. Egypt

The End - GENESIS

EXODUS

1. Exodus 1:1
Answer - a. children of Israel   b. Jacob

2. Exodus 1:6
Answer - a. and all that generation

3. Exodus 1:9
Answer - a. are more and mightier than we

4. Exodus 1:13
Answer - a. the children of Israel

5. Exodus 1:22
Answer - a. every son that is born ye shall cast into the river

6. Exodus 2:6
Answer - a. she saw the child b. the babe wept c. the Hebrews' children

7. Exodus 2:10
Answer - a. Pharaoh's daughter and he became her son b. Moses c. because I drew him out of the water

8. Exodus 2:12
Answer - a. he slew the Egyptian and hid him in the sand

9. Exodus 2:15
Answer - a. he sought to slay Moses,   b. from the face of Pharaoh

10. Exodus 2:21-22
Answer - a. and he gave Moses Zipporah his daughter   b. Gershon   c. a strange land

11. Exodus 2:24
Answer - a. Abraham, with Isaac and with Jacob

12. Exodus 3:1
Answer - a. and he led the flock to the backside of the desert

13. Exodus 3:3
Answer - a. why the bush is not burnt

14. Exodus 3:5
Answer - a. put off thy shoes from off thy feet, for the place whereon thy standest is holy ground

15. Exodus 3:10
Answer - a. bring forth my people the children of Israel out of Egypt

16. Exodus 3:14
Answer - a. I AM hath sent me unto you

17. Exodus 3:16-17
Answer - a. I have surely visited you and seen that which is done to you in Egypt   b. I will bring you up out of the affiction of Egypt   c. unto a land flowing with milk and honey

18. Exodus 3:20
Answer - a. with all my wonders   b. after that he will let you go

19. Exodus 4:2
Answer - a. a rod

20. Exodus 4:10
Answer - a. I am not eloquent   b. but I am slow of speech, and of a slow tongue

21. Exodus 4:12
Answer - a. mouth, and teach thee what thou shall say

22. Exodus 4:14
Answer - a. is not Aaron the Levite thy brother? I know that he can speak well   b. he will be glad in his heart

23. Exodus 4:16
Answer - a. spokesman unto the people   b. thou shalt be to him instead of God

24. Exodus 4:20
Answer - a. and returned to the land of Egypt   b. the rod of God in his hand

25. Exodus 4:30
Answer - a. which the Lord had spoken unto Moses

26. Exodus 5:1-2
Answer - a. let my people go   b. that I should obey his voice to let Israel go?   C. neither will I let Israel go

27. Exodus 5:23
Answer - a. neither hast thou delivered thy people at all

28. Exodus 6:2-4
Answer - a. the Lord b. God Almighty c. Jehovah was I not known to them   d. Covenant   e. wherein they were strangers

29. Exodus 7:1
Answer - a. and Aaron thy brother shall be thy prophet

30. Exodus 7:10
Answer - a. and it became a serpent

31. Exodus 7:12
Answer - a. Aaron's rod swallowed up their rods

32. Exodus 7:20
Answer - a. in the sight of Pharaoh   b. and all the water that were in the river were turned to blood

33. Exodus 8:5
Answer - a. strecth forth thine hand with thy rod   b. cause frogs to come up upon the land of Egypt

34. Exodus 8:16
Answer - a. that it may become lice throughout all the land of Egypt

35. Exodus 8:24
Answer - a. there came a grievous swarm of flies   b. the land was corrupted by reason of the swarm of flies

36. Exodus 9:6
Answer - a. but of the cattle of the children of Israel died not one

37. Exodus 9:9
Answer - a. be a boil breaking forth with blains upon man

38. Exodus 9:18
Answer - a. I will cause it to rain a very grievous hail

39. Exodus 10:12
Answer - a. for the locusts   b. eat every herb of the land even all that the hail hath left

40. Exodus 10:21
Answer - a. toward heaven, that there may be darkness

41. Exodus 11:10
Answer - a. so that he would not let the children of Israel go out of his land

42. Exodus 12:7
Answer - a. the two side post and on the upper door post of the house

43. Exodus 12:13
Answer - a. a token upon the house where ye are: and when I see the blood, I will pass over you

44. Exodus 12:24
Answer - a. for ever

45. Exodus 12:27
Answer - a. it is the sacrifice of the Lord's Passover   b. and the people bowed the head and worshipped

46. Exodus 12:29
Answer - a. firstborn of Pharaoh   b. all the firstborn of cattle

47. Exodus 12:30
Answer - a. for there was not a house where there was not one dead

48. Exodus 12:31
Answer - a. rise up, and get you forth from among my people   b. serve the Lord

49. Exodus 12:35-36
Answer - a. Moses   b. favour in the sight of the Egyptians   c. such things as they required

50. Exodus 12:51
Answer - a. children of Israel

51. Exodus 13:1-2
Answer - a. firstborn   b. the children of Israel   c. it is mine

52. Exodus 13:16
Answer - a. token   b. for thy strength of hand   c. out of Egypt

53. Exodus 13:19
Answer - a. the bones of Joseph with him   b. and ye shall carry up my bones away hence with you

54. Exodus 13:21
Answer - a. in a pillar of cloud   b. in a pillar of fire

55. Exodus 14:4
Answer - a. that he shall follow after them   b. may know   c. I AM

56. Exodus 14:13-14
Answer - a. fear ye not, stand still and see the salvation of the Lord   b. no more for ever   c. and ye shall hold your peace

57. Exodus 14:21-22
Answer - a. east wind   b. made the sea dry land   c. the children of Israel   d. dry ground   e. right hand and on their left

58. Exodus 14: 28
Answer - a. there remained not so much as one of them

59. Exodus 15:1
Answer - a. I will sing unto the Lord, for he hath triumphed gloriously; the horse and his rider hath been thrown into the sea

60. Exodus 15:20
Answer - a. the sister of Aaron   b. with timbrel and with dances

61. Exodus 15:24-25
Answer - a. what shall we drink?   b. Lord showed him a tree   c. the water was made sweet

62. Exodus 15:26
Answer - a. and wilt do that which is right in his sight   b. diseases upon thee   c. for I AM the Lord that healeth thee

63. Exodus 16:4
Answer - a. I will rain bread from heaven for you   b. that I may prove them

64. Exodus 16:8
Answer - a. your murmuring are not against us, but against the Lord

65. Exodus 16:26
Answer - a. Sabbath in it there shall be none

66. Exodus 17:6
Answer - a. and there shall come water out of it

67. Exodus 18:13
Answer - a. stood by Moses from the morning unto the evening

68. Exodus 18:15-16
Answer - a. because the people come unto me to inquire of God   b. and I judge between one and another

69. Exodus 18:25-26
Answer - a. the hard causes they brought unto Moses

70. Exodus 19:3-6
Answer - a. Lord called unto him   b. and how I bare you on eagles' wings, and brought you unto myself   c. covenant   d. peculiar treasure   e. these are the words which thou shalt speak unto the children of Israel

71. Exodus 20:18
Answer - a. thundering   b. lightings   c. trumpet   d. smoking

72. Exodus 20: 2-17
Answer - a. READ/LIST/UNDERLINE THE TEN COMMANDMENTS

73. Exodus 20:22
Answer - a. ye have seen that I have talked with you from heaven

74. Exodus 21:15
Answer - a. shall be surely put to death

75. Exodus 22:4
Answer - a. he shall restore double

76. Exodus 23:22
Answer - a. obey his voice, and do all that I speak

77. Exodus 24:1
Answer - a. thou and Aaron, Nadab, and Abihu and

78. Exodus 24:3-4
Answer - a. all the words which the Lord hath said will we do   b. twelve pillars,   c. the twelve tribes of Israel

79. Exodus 24:8
Answer - a. sprinkled it on the people, and said, behold, the blood of the covenant

80: Exodus 24:18
Answer - a. and Moses was in the mount forty days and forty nights

81. Exodus 25:2
Answer - a. bring me an offering

82. Exodus 25:6
Answer - a. spices for anointing oil

83. Exodus 25:23
Answer - a. table of shillin wood   b. and a cubit and a half the height thereof

84. Exodus 26:1
Answer - a. with cherubims of cunning work shalt thou make them

85. Exodus 26:14
Answer - a. of rams skin dyed red   b. of badgers skins

86. Exodus 27:1
Answer - a. an altar   b. shall be three cubits

87. Exodus 27:8
Answer - a. as it was shown thee in the mount

88. Exodus 28:2
Answer - a. for Aaron thy brother for glory and for beauty

89. Exodus 28:9-10
Answer - a. the names of the children of Israel   b. according to their birth

90. Exodus 28:41
Answer - a. and shalt anoint them, and consecrate them, and sanctify them   b. priest's office

91. Exodus 29:7
Answer - a. anointing oil, and pour it upon his head

92. Exodus 29:33
Answer - a. the atonement was made, to consecrate and to sanctify them

93. Exodus 29:46
Answer - a. I AM the Lord their God   b. I AM the Lord their God

94. Exodus 30:15
Answer - a. and the poor shall not give less than half a shekel   b. atonement

95. Exodus 31:3
Answer - a. with the spirit of God

96. Exodus 31:13
Answer - a. for it is a sign between me and you

97. Exodus 32:3
Answer - a. and brought them unto Aaron

98. Exodus 32:7
Answer - a. go, get thee down   b. have corrupted themselves

99. Exodus 32:9
Answer - a. it is a stiffnecked people

100. Exodus 32:14
Answer - a. repented   b. do unto his people

101. Exodus 32:19
Answer - a. he saw the calf, and the dancing   b. brake them beneath the mount

102. Exodus 32:26
Answer - a. who is on the Lord's side?   b. all the sons of Levi

103. Exodus 32:33
Answer - a. him will I blot out of my book

104. Exodus 33:7
Answer - a. the tabernacles   b. the tabernacles of the congregation

105. Exodus 33:17
Answer - a. for thou hast found grace in my sight, and I know thee by name

106. Exodus 34:1
Answer - a. which thou brakest

107. Exodus 34:14
Answer - a. is a jealous God

108. Exodus 34:20
Answer - a. firstling   b. if thou redeem him not   c. firstborn   d. and none shall appear before me empty

109. Exodus 34:27-30
Answer - a. I have made a covenant with thee and with Israel   b. forty days and forty nights   c. upon the tables the word of the covenant, the ten commandments   d. Mount Sinai   e. the skin of his face shone while he talked with him   f. the skin of his face shone

110. Exodus 34:33
Answer - a. he put a veil on his face

111. Exodus 35:1
Answer - a. commanded that ye should do them

112. Exodus 35:30-31
Answer - a. Bezabeel the son of Uri, the son of Hur, of the tribe of Judah   b. him with the spirit of God

113. Exodus 35:34
Answer - a. in his heart that he may teach   b. the tribe of Dan

114. Exodus 36:5
Answer - a. the people bring much more than enough

115. Exodus 36:38
Answer - a. but their five sockets were of brass

116. Exodus 37:23
Answer - a. of pure gold

117. Exodus 37:29
Answer - a. the holy anointing oil

118. Exodus 38:21
Answer - a. for the service of the Levites   b. Ithamar son of Aaron the priest

119. Exodus 38:22
Answer - a. Uri   b. Hur, of the tribe of Judah

120. Exodus 39:1
Answer - a. and make the holy garments for Aaron   b . Moses

121. Exodus 39:32
Answer - a. Moses, so did they

122. Exodus 39:43
Answer - a. and behold, they had done it as the Lord had commanded   b. and Moses blessed them

123. Exodus 40:31-34
Answer - a. washed their hands and their feet thereat b. went into   c. came near   d. they washed   e. hanging of the court gate   f. and the glory of the Lord filled the tabernacle

124. Exodus 40:38
Answer - a. by day and fire was on it by night

The End - EXODUS

LEVITICUS

1. Leviticus 1:3-4
Answer - a. let him offer a male without blemish   b. before the Lord   c. accepted for him to make atonement for him

2. Leviticus 2:1
Answer - a. shall be of fine flour; and he shall pour oil upon it

3. Leviticus 2:12
Answer - a. firstfruit, ye shall offer them unto the Lord

4. Leviticus 3:1
Answer - a. peace offering   b. without blemish before the Lord

5. Leviticus 4:3
Answer - a. according to the sin of the people   b. for a sin offering

6. Leviticus 5:17
Answer - a. and shall bear his iniquity

7. Leviticus 6:7
Answer - a. atonement for him   b. in trespassing therein

8. Leviticus 7:31
Answer - a. Aaron's and his sons

9. Leviticus 8:10
Answer - a. and anointed the tabernacle   b. and sanctified them

10. Leviticus 8:12
Answer - a. Aaron's head, and anointed him

11. Leviticus 9:8
Answer - a. which was for himself

12. Leviticus 9:22
Answer - a. toward the people and blessed them   b. sin   c. burnt   d. peace offerings

13. Leviticus 10:1-2
Answer - a. sons of Aaron   b. strange fire   c. which he commanded them not   d. devoured them, and they died before the Lord

14. Leviticus 10:12
Answer - a. his sons that were left   b. for it is most holy

15. Leviticus 11:9
Answer - a. fins and scales   b. them shall ye eat

16. Leviticus 11:45
Answer - a. for I AM holy

17. Leviticus 12:2-3
Answer - a. if a woman have conceived seed, and born a man child: then   b. the flesh of his foreskin shall be circumcised

18. Leviticus 13:3
Answer - a. and when the hair in the plague is turned white,   b. it is a plague of leprosy   c. unclean

19. Leviticus 13:13
Answer - a. if the leprosy have covered all his flesh   b.   he is clean

20: Leviticus 13:59
Answer - a. to pronounce it clean or to pronounce it unclean

21. Leviticus 14:8
Answer - a. come into the camp   b. seven days

22. Leviticus 14:34-35
Answer - a. Moses   b. Aaron   c. the land of canaan   d. plague of leprosy   e. come and tell the priest
f. a plague in the house

23. Leviticus 14:57
Answer - a. unclean   b. clean

24. Leviticus 15:12
Answer - a. and every vessel of wood shall be rinsed in water

25. Leviticus 15:15
Answer - a. an atonement

26. Leviticus 15:28
Answer - a. number to herself seven days

27. Leviticus 16:16
Answer - a. uncleanness of the children of Israel   b. transgressions in all their sins

28. Leviticus 16:30-31
Answer - a. make an atonement for you   b. from all your sins   c. Sabbath of rest unto you

29. Leviticus 16:34
Answer - a. everlasting statue unto you   b. children of Israel   c. once a year

30. Leviticus 17:6
Answer - a. upon the altar of the Lord   b. tabernacle of the congregation

31. Leviticus 17:16
Answer - a. then he shall bear his iniquity

32. Leviticus 18:5
Answer - a. which if a man do

33. Leviticus 18:6
Answer - a. that is near of kin to him

34. Leviticus 18:20
Answer - a. to defile thyself with her

35. Leviticus 9: 1-2
Answer - a. the congregation   b. holy   c. holy

36. Leviticus 19:5
Answer - a. at your own will

37. Leviticus 19:11
Answer - a. neither lie one to another

38. Leviticus 20:13
Answer - a. as he lieth with a woman

39. Leviticus 20:26
Answer - a. holy   b. that ye should be mine

40. Leviticus 21:4
Answer - a. being a chief man among his people

41. Leviticus 21:24
Answer - a. unto all the children of Israel

42. Leviticus 22:8
Answer - a. he shall not eat to defile himself therewith

43. Leviticus 22:33
Answer - a. the land of Egypt

44. Leviticus 23:2
Answer - a. the feast of the Lord   b. holy convocation

45. Leviticus 23:9-10
Answer - a. when ye be come into the land which I give unto you   b. sheaf of the firstfruit of your harvest unto the priest

46. Leviticus 23:28
Answer - a. for it is a day of atonement   b. Lord your God

47. Leviticus 23:44
Answer - a. the children of Israel

48. Leviticus 24:2
Answer - a. pure oil olive beaten   b. continually

49. Leviticus 25:2-4
Answer - a. keep a Sabbath unto the Lord,   b. six years   c. seventh year   d. Sabbath of rest   e. Sabbath

50. Leviticus 25:9
Answer - a. the tenth day of the seventh month

51. Leviticus 25:21
Answer - a. blessing upon you in the sixth year

52. Leviticus 25:55
Answer - a. they are my servants

53. Leviticus 26:2
Answer - a. and reverence my sanctuary

54. Leviticus 26:2-4
Answer - a. and do them   b. due season c. increase

55. Leviticus 26:8-9
Answer - a. chase an hundred   b. ten thousands to flight   c. respect unto you   d. and establish my covenant with you

56. Leviticus 26:13
Answer - a. I have broken the bands of your yoke

57. Leviticus 26:24
Answer - a. seven times for your sins

58. Leviticus 26:40-42
Answer - a. they have walked contrary unto me   b. if then their uncircumcised hearts be humbled,   c. remember my covenant with Jacob, and also my covenant with Isaac and also my covenant with Abraham will I remember

59. Leviticus 27:1-2
Answer - a. when a man shall make a singular vow

60. Leviticus 27:26
Answer - a. which should be the Lord's firstling   b. it is the Lord's

61. Leviticus 27:30
Answer - a. is the Lord's : it is holy unto the Lord

62. Leviticus 27: 32
Answer - a. the tenth shall be holy unto the Lord

63. Leviticus 27:34
Answer - a. Moses

THE END - LEVITICUS

NUMBERS

1. Numbers 1:1-4
Answer - a. in the wilderness of Sinai   b. in the second year   c. with the number of their names   d. thou and Aaron shall number them by their armies   e. of every tribe

2. Numbers 1:46-47
Answer - a. six hundred thousand and three thousand and five hundred and fifty

3. Numbers 1:50
Answer - a. appoint the Levites over the tabernacle of testimony

4. Numbers 2:2
Answer - a. pitch by his own standard   b. shall they pitch

5. Numbers 2:22
Answer - a. Abidan the son of Gideon

6. Numbers 3:4
Answer - a. died before the Lord, when they offered strange fire   b. Aaron their father

7. Numbers 3:7
Answer - a. and the charge   b. the service of the tabernacle

8. Numbers 3:28
Answer - a. keeping the charge of the sanctuary

9. Numbers 3:42
Answer - a. all the firstborn among

10. Numbers 3:49
Answer - a. the redemption money   b. Levites

11. Numbers 4:4
Answer - a. sons of Kohath   b. the most holy things

12. Numbers 4:34
Answer - a. chief of the congregation

13. Numbers 4:49
Answer - a. they were numbered by the hand of Moses   b. as the Lord commanded Moses

14. Numbers 5:2
Answer - a. every leper, and every one that hath an issue

15. Numbers 5:23
Answer - a. and he shall blot them out

16. Numbers 5:31
Answer - a. shall bear her iniquity

17. Numbers 6:2-3
Answer - a. to vow a vow of a Nazarite   b. wine and strong drinks   c. nor eat moist grapes or dried

18. Numbers 6:5
Answer - a. shall no razor come upon his head   b. of his head grow

19. Numbers 6:6
Answer - a. no dead body

20. Numbers 6:8
Answer - a. holy unto the Lord

21. Numbers 6:13
Answer - a. when the days of his separation are fulfilled   b. tabernacle of the congregation

22. Numbers 7:9
Answer - a. he gave none   b. bear upon their shoulders

23. Numbers 7:30
Answer - a. prince of the children of Reuben, did offer

24. Numbers 7:60
Answer - a. prince of the children of Benjamin, offered

25. Numbers 7:78
Answer - a. Naphtali, offered

26. Numbers 8:2
Answer - a. the seven lamps shall give light over against

27. Numbers 8:21
Answer - a. and Aaron made an atonement for them to cleanse them

28. Numbers 8:25
Answer - a. fifty years   b. and shall serve no more

29. Numbers 9:2
Answer - a. the Passover at his appointed season

30. Numbers 9:8
Answer - a. stand still   b. concerning you

31. Numbers 9:16
Answer - a. of fire by night

32. Numbers 10:3
Answer - a. all the assembly shall assemble themselves to thee

33. Numbers 10:12
Answer - a. the wilderness of Sinai

34. Numbers 10:17
Answer - a. bearing the tabernacle

35. Numbers 10:35
Answer - a. and let them that hate thee flee before thee

36. Numbers 11:1
Answer - a. complained   b. and his anger was kindled   c. and consumed them that were

37. Numbers 11:14
Answer - a. because it is too heavy for me

38. Numbers 11:16
Answer - a. seventy men of the elders of Israel

39. Numbers 11:28
Answer - a. my Lord Moses, forbid them

40. Number 11:33-34
Answer - a. yet between their teeth   b. buried the people that lusted

41. Numbers 12:1
Answer - a. because of the Ethiopian woman whom he had married

42. Numbers 12:5
Answer - a. and called Aaron and Miriam

43. Numbers 12:9
Answer - a. was kindled against them

44. Numbers 12:10
Answer - a. Miriam became leprous, white as snow   b. she was leprous

45. Numbers 12:15
Answer - a. seven days   b. Miriam was brought in again

46. Numbers 13:3
Answer - a. all those men were heads of the children of Israel

47. Numbers 13:17
Answer - a. the land of Canaan

48. Numbers 13:25
Answer - a. after forty days

49. Numbers 13:27
Answer - a. surely it floweth with milk and honey

50. Numbers 13:32-33
Answer - a. is a land that eateth up the inhabitants thereof   b. are men of great stature   c. giants   d. as grasshoppers

51. Numbers 14:35-38
Answer - a. that are gathered together against me   b. and made all the congregation to murmur against me
c. evil report upon the land, died by the plague   d. Joshua   e. Caleb   f. lived still

52. Numbers 15:12
Answer - a. every one according to their number

53. Numbers 15:16
Answer - a. stranger that sojourned with you

54. Numbers 15:28
Answer - a. soul that sinneth ignorantly   b. and it shall be forgiven him

55. Numbers 15:33
Answer - a. Moses and Aaron, and unto all the congregation

56. Numbers 15:40
Answer - a. and be holy unto your God

57. Numbers 16:19-20
Answer - a. and the glory of the Lord appeared unto all the congregation   b. that I may consume them in a moment

58. Numbers 16:32
Answer - a. swallowed them up

59. Numbers 17:3
Answer - a. Aaron's name upon the rod of Levi   b. one rod

60. Numbers 17:5
Answer - a. shall blossom

61. Numbers 17:7-8
Answer - a. rods   b. the rod of Aaron for the house of Levi was budded   c. yielded almonds

62. Numbers 17:10
Answer - a. to be kept as a token against the rebels,

63. Numbers 18:6
Answer - a. to do the service of the tabernacle of the congregation

64. Numbers 18:12
Answer - a. the firstfruit of them which they shall offer unto the Lord

65. Numbers 18:21
Answer - a. for their service which they service

66. Numbers 18:26
Answer - a. the tithes   b. from them for your inheritance   c. even a tenth part of the tithe

67. Numbers 19:4
Answer - a. seven times

68. Numbers 19:9
Answer - a. clean place   b. it is a purification for sin

69. Numbers 20:1
Answer - a. Miriam died there, and was buried there

70. Numbers 20:11
Answer - a. smote the rock twice

71. Numbers 20:12
Answer - a. therefore ye shall not

72. Numbers 20:24
Answer - a. for he shall not enter into the land

73. Numbers 20:28
Answer - a. and Aaron died there in the top of the mount

74. Numbers 21:6
Answer - a. people of Israel died

75. Numbers 21:8-9
Answer - a. set it upon a pole   b. shall live   c. he lived

76. Numbers 21:17
Answer - a. spring up, O well, sing ye unto it

77. Numbers 21:34
Answer - a. for I have delivered him into thy hand

78. Numbers 22:11
Answer - a. come now, curse me them   b. drive them out

79. Numbers 22:21-23
Answer - a. kindled because he went   b. angel of the Lord standing in the way   c. and Balaam smote the ass, to turn into the way

80. Numbers 22:33
Answer - a. surely now also I had slain thee, and saved her alive

81. Numbers 23:8
Answer - a. not curse?   b. not defied?

82. Numbers 23:20
Answer - a. I cannot reverse it

83. Numbers 23:26
Answer - a. that I must do

84. Numbers 24:2
Answer - a. and the Spirit of God came upon him

85. Numbers 24:15-16
Answer - a. the knowledge of the most high   b. falling into a trance

86. Numbers 25:8-9
Answer - a. the man of Israel, and the woman through her belly   b. twenty and four thousand

87. Number 26:1-2
Answer - a. sum of all the congregation

88. Numbers 26:52-53
Answer - a. for an inheritance

89. Numbers 26:64
Answer - a. was not a man   b. numbered

90. Numbers 27:6-7
Answer - a. Zekiohehad speak right   b. of their father to pass unto them

91. 27:12-13
Answer - a. Moses   b. and see the land   c. thou also shalt be gathered unto thy people

92. Numbers 27:15-16
Answer - a. the God of the spirit of all flesh

93. Numbers 27:22-23
Answer - a. Joshua, and set him before Eleazar the priest   b. laid his hand upon him

94. Numbers 28:1-2
Answer - a. my offering, and my bread for my sacrifices made by fire

95. Numbers 28:13
Answer - a. a sacrifice made by fire unto the Lord

96. Numbers 29:1
Answer - a. ye shall have an holy convocation

97. Numbers 29:39
Answer - a. beside your vows and your freewill offerings

98. Numbers 30:2
Answer - a. he shall not break his word,   b. proceeded out of his mouth

99. Numbers 31:7
Answer - a. and they slew all the males

100. Numbers 31:23
Answer - a. nevertheless it shall be purified with the water of separation

101. Numbers 31:27
Answer - a. congregation

102. Numbers 31:54
Answer - a. for a memorial

103. Numbers 32:10-13
Answer - a. unto Abraham, unto Isaac and unto Jacob   b. Caleb   c. and Joshua   d. wholly followed the Lord   e. forty years   f. was consumed

104. Numbers 32:29
Answer - a. Gad   b. Reuben   c. over Jordan

105. Numbers 32:30
Answer - a. land of Canaan

106. Numbers 33:2
Answer - a. are their journeys according to their goings out

107. Numbers 33:52
Answer - a. all their high places

108. Numbers 33:55
Answer - a. pricks in your eyes, and throns in your sides

109. Numbers 34:1-2
Answer - a. the land of Canaan

110. Numbers 34:17
Answer - a. Eleazar the priest and Joshua the son of Dan

111. Numbers 34:29
Answer - a. Canaan

112. Number 35:4
Answer - a. Levites

113. Numbers 35:14
Answer - a. which shall be cities of refuge

114. Numbers 35:34
Answer - a. for I the Lord dwell among

115. Numbers 36:6
Answer - a. daughters of Zelophehad   b. shall they marry

116. Numbers 36:13
Answer - a. Moses   b. Jericho

THE END - NUMBERS

DEUTERONOMY

1. Deuteronomy 1:3
Answer - a. that Moses spake unto the children of Israel

2. Deuteronomy 1:8
Answer - a. sware unto your father

3. Deuteronomy 1:32-33
Answer - a. believe the Lord your God   b, in fire by night   c. in a cloud by day

4. Deuteronomy 1:42
Answer - a. go not up   b. for I am not among your enemies

5. Deuteronomy 1:44
Answer - a. and chased you, as bees do.

6. Deuteronomy 2:5
Answer - a. because I have given mount Seir unto Esau for a possession

7. Deuteronomy 2:7
Answer - a. blessed thee   b. thou hast lacked nothing

8. Deuteronomy 2:15
Answer - a. until they were consumed

9. Deuteronomy 2:33
Answer - a. and we smote him and his sons

10. Deuteronomy 3:3
Answer - a. none was left to him remaining

11. Deuteronomy 3:28
Answer - a. Joshua   b. and he shall cause them to inherit the land

12. Deuteronomy 4:2
Answer - a. neither shall ye diminish aught from it

13. Deuteronomy 4:6
Answer - a. your wisdom and your understanding

14. Deuteronomy 4:13
Answer - a. covenant   b. he wrote them upon two tables of stones

15. Deuteronomy 4:22
Answer - a. I must not go over Jordan

16. Deuteronomy 4:29
Answer - a. if thou seek him with all thy heart and with all thy soul

17. Deuteronomy 4:31
Answer - a. he will not forsake thee   b. nor forget the covenant of thy fathers

18. Deuteronomy 4:35
Answer - a. there is none else beside him

19. Deuteronomy 4:37
Answer - a. mighty power

20. Deuteronomy 4:39
Answer - a. in heaven above

21. Deuteronomy 5:1-3
Answer - a. hear O Israel   b. covenent   c. made not this covenant with our fathers

22. Deuteronomy 5:22
Answer - a. great voice   b. two tables of stones

23. Deuteronomy 5:33
Answer - a. and that ye may prolong your days

24. Deuteronomy 6:3-6
Answer - a. and that ye may increase mightly   b. in the land that floweth with milk and honey   c. is one Lord

25. Deuteronomy 6:18
Answer - a. in the sight of the Lord

26. Deuteronomy 7:6
Answer - a. special people unto himself

27. Deuteronomy 7:9
Answer - a. covenant and mercy   b. to a thousand generations

28. Deuteronomy 7:15
Answer - a. all sickness   b. upon thee   c. hate thee

29. Deuteronomy 8:2
Answer - a. remember   b. forty years   c. to humble thee, and to prove thee

30. Deuteronomy 8:6
Answer - a. to walk in his ways, and to fear him

31. Deuteronomy 8:18
Answer - a. for it is he that giveth thee power to get wealth   b. covenant   c. as it is this day

32. Deuteronomy 9:20-21
Answer - a. Aaron to have destroyed him   b. the calf which ye had made   c. even until it was as small as dust   d. dust

33. Deuteronomy 10:4
Answer - a. the ten commandments   c. out of the midst of the fire

34. Deuteronomy 10:16
Answer - a. and be no more stiffnecked

35. Deuteronomy 10:19
Answer - a. for ye were strangers in the land of Egypt

36. Deuteronomy 11:6
Answer - a. Reuben: how the earth opened her mouth and swallowed them up   b. in the midst of all Israel

37. Deuteronomy 11:18
Answer - a. words   b. they may be as frontlet between your eyes

38. Deuteronomy 11:32
Answer - a. statutes and judgments

39. Deuteronomy 12:6
Answer - a. burnt offering   b. sacrifices   c. tithes   d. heave offerings   e. vows   f. freewill offering g. firstling

40. Deuteronomy 12:28
Answer - a. and with thy children after thee for ever

41. Deuteronomy 12:32
Answer - a. thou shalt not add thereto nor diminish from it

42. Deuteronomy 13:3
Answer - a. that prophet or that dreamer of dreams

43. Deuteronomy 14:6
Answer - a. that ye shall eat

44. Deuteronomy 14:19
Answer - a. unclean   b. they shall not be eaten

45. Deuteronomy 15:1
Answer - a. every seven years   b. release

46. Deuteronomy 15:6
Answer - a. thou shall lend unto many nations, but thou shall not borrow   b. but they shall not reigh over thee

47. Deuteronomy 15:13
Answer - a. thou shall not let him go away empty

48. Deuteronomy 16:1
Answer - a. out of Egypt by night

49. Deuteronomy 16:9
Answer - a. put the sickle to the corn

50. Deuteronomy 16:13
Answer - a. seven days

51. Deuteronomy 16:20
Answer - a. altogether just

52. Deuteronomy 17:6
Answer - a. he shall not be put to death

53. Deuteronomy 17:18
Answer - a. sitteth upon the throne of his kingdom

54. Deuteronomy 18:15
Answer - a. a prophet from the midst of thee

55. Deuteronomy 18:22
Answer - a. follow not, nor come to pass   b. not spoken

56. Deuteronomy 19:20
Answer - a. no more any such evil among you

57. Deuteronomy 20:4
Answer - a. to save you

58. Deuteronomy 21:1
Answer - a. who hath slain him

59. Deuteronomy 21:7
Answer - a. neither have our eyes seen it

60. Deuteronomy 21:17
Answer - a. the firstborn, by giving him a double portion of all that he hath

61. Deuteronomy 22:5
Answer - a. for all that do so are abomination unto the Lord thy God

62. Deuteronomy 22:30
Answer - a. nor discover his father's skirt

63. Deuteronomy 23:23
Answer - a. vowed   b. which thou hast promised with thy mouth

64. Deuteronomy 24:9
Answer - a. Miriam

65. Deuteronomy 24:16
Answer - a. every man shall be put to death for his own sin

66. Deuteronomy 25:1
Answer - a. shall justify the righteous, and condemn the wicked

67. Deuteronomy 25:10
Answer - a. hath his shoe loosed

68. Deuteronomy 26:2
Answer - a. and shalt put it in a basket

69. Deuteronomy 26:10
Answer - a. firstfruits   b. O Lord hast given me

70. Deuteronomy 26:12
Answer - a. which is the year of tithing   b. Levites, the stranger, the fatherless and the widow

71. Deuteronomy 26:15
Answer - a. and bless thy people Israel   b. a land that floweth with milk and honey

72. Deuteronomy 27:9-10
Answer - a. take heed, and hearken O Israel   b. obey the voice of the Lord thy God

73. Deuteronomy 27:20
Answer - a. father's wife   b. skirt   c. AMEN

74. Deuteronomy 28:1-2
Answer - a. voice   b. will set thee on high above all nations of the earth   c. and overtake thee   d. voice

75. Deuteronomy 28:6
Answer - a. thou comest in   b. thou goest out

76. Deuteronomy 28:7
Answer - a. against thee one way, and flee before thee seven ways

77. Deuteronomy 28:13
Answer - a. and not the tail   b. above only   c. not be beneath   d. to do them

78. Deuteronomy 28:15
Answer - a. not.   b. voice   c. to do all   d. curses shall come upon thee, and overtake thee

79. Deuteronomy 28:62
Answer - a. as the stars of heaven for multitude   b. voice

80. Deuteronomy 29:1
Answer - a. children of Israel   b. the covenant which he made with them in Horeb

81. Deuteronomy 29:9
Answer - a. that ye may prosper in all that ye do

82. Deuteronomy 29:29
Answer - a. but those things which are revealed belong unto us

83. Deuteronomy 30:19
Answer - a. therefore choose life, that both thou and thy seed may live

84. Deuteronomy 30:20
Answer - a. obey his voice   b. for he is thy life, and the length of thy days   c. to Abraham, to Isaac, and to Jacob

85. Deuteronomy 31:1-2
Answer - a. I can no more go out and come in   b. thou shalt not go over this Jordan

86. Deuteronomy 31:7
Answer - a. be strong and of good courage   b. and thou shall cause them to inherit it

87. Deuteronomy 31:14
Answer - a. must die   b. Joshua   c. that I may give him a charge

88. Deuteronomy 31:25-26
Answer - a. which bare the ark of the covenant   b. put it in the side of the ark of the covenant

89. Deuteronomy 32:3
Answer - a. greatness unto our God

90. Deuteronomy 32:7
Answer - a. and he will show thee   b. they will tell thee

91. Deuteronomy 32:44
Answer - a. the son of Nun

92. Deuteronomy 32:48-52
Answer - a. unto mount Nebo   b. that is over against Jericho   c. die   d. died in mount Hor   e. in the wilderness of Zin   f. but thou shalt not go thither unto the land

93. Deuteronomy 33:1

Answer - a. before his death

94. Deuteronomy 33:13

Answer - a. precious things of heaven

95. Deuteronomy 34:4-5

Answer - a. but thou shalt not go over thither.   So Moses the servant of the Lord died there in the land of Moah

96. Deuteronomy 34:9

Answer - a. full of the spirit of wisdom   b. and the children of Israel

97. Deuteronomy 34:10

Answer - a. Moses

THE END - DEUTERONOMY

NEW TESTAMENT ANSWERS

1. St. Matt. 1:2
Answer - a. Judas and all his brethren

2. St. Matt. 1:16
Answer - a. Jesus   b. Christ

3. St. Matt. 1:17
Answer - a. fourteen generations   b. fourteen generations   c. fourteen generations

4. St. Matt. 1:18
Answer - a. she was found with child of the Holy Ghost

5. St. Matt. 1:19-20
Answer - a. being a just man   b. thou son of David   c. is of the Holy Ghost

6. St. Matt. 1:22-23
Answer - a. fulfilled   b. Emmanuel   c. God with us

7. St. Matt. 1:25
Answer - a. firstborn son   b. Jesus

8. St. Matt. 2:1
Answer - a. Bethlehem   b. Herod   c. from the east

9. St. Matt. 2:3
Answer - a. he was troubled

10. St. Matt. 2:12
Answer - a. not return to Herod   b. departed   c. another way

11. St. Matt. 2:13
Answer - a. the angel of the Lord   b. dream   c. to destroy him

12. St. Matt. 2:19-20
Answer - a. Joseph in Egypt   b. the young child's life

13. St. Matt. 2:22-23
Answer - a. being warned of God in a dream   b. Nazareth   c. Nazarene

14. St. Matt. 3:1
Answer - a. Preaching   b. Judaea

15. St. Matt. 3:3
Answer - a. the voice of one crying in the wilderness

16. St. Matt. 3:4
Answer - a. locusts and wild honey

17. St. Matt. 3:11
Answer - a. mightier than I   b. Holy Ghost and with fire

18. St. Matt. 3:13
Answer - a. baptized

19. St. Matt. 3:16-17
Answer - a. lo, the heavens were opened unto him   b. like a dove, and lighting upon him   c. in whom I am well pleased.

20. St. Matt. 4:1-2
Answer - a. forty days   b. forty nights

21. St. Matt. 4:7
Answer - a. thou shall not tempt

22. St. Matt. 4:10
Answer - a. thou shalt worship the Lord thy God

23. St. Matt. 4:11
Answer - a. ministered unto him

24. St. Matt. 4:12
Answer - a. cast, into prison   b. Galilee

25. St. Matt. 4:17
Answer - a. repent

26. St. Matt. 4:19
Answer - a. follow me

27. St. Matt. 4:21-22
Answer - a. immediately   b. followed him

28. St. Matt. 4:23
Answer - a. healing   b. disease

29. St. Matt. 5:1-2
Answer - a. mountain   b. disciples

30. St. Matt. 5:3
Answer - a. kingdom of heaven

31. St. Matt. 5:7
Answer - a. mercy

32. St. Matt. 5:11
Answer - a. manner of evil against you falsely

33. St. Matt. 5:16
Answer - a. Verse 16   b. glorify

34. St. Matt. 5:22
Answer - a. Verse 22

35. St. Matt. 5:34
Answer - a. Verse 34   b. God's throne

36. St. Matt. 5:45
Answer - a. maketh his sun to rise on the evil   b. just and on the unjust

37. St. Matt. 6:9-13
Answer - a. Verse 9-13

38. St. Matt. 6:24
Answer - a. ye cannot serve God and Mammon

39. St. Matt. 6:33
Answer - a. seek   b. righteousness   c. added

40. St. Matt. 7:1
Answer - a. not

41. St. Matt. 7:7
Answer - a. given   b. seek   c. knock

42. St. Matt. 7:15
Answer - a. ravening wolves

43. St. Matt. 7:20
Answer - a. fruits

44. St. Matt. 7:27
Answer - a. floods came   b. winds blew   c. it fell

45. St. Matt. 8:13
Answer - a. believed   b. selfsame hour

46. St. Matt. 8:23-27
Answer - a. followed him   b. tempest in the sea   c. covered with the waves   d. Lord, save us: we perish
e. O ye of little faith   f. great calm   g. what manner of man is this   h. obey him

47. St. Matt. 9:2
Answer - a. seeing their faith   b. thy sins be forgiven thee

48. St. Matt. 9:9
Answer - a. Matthew   b. follow me   c. followed him

49. St. Matt. 9:13
Answer - a. but sinners to repentance

50. St. Matt. 9:18-22
Answer - a. there came a certain ruler   b. now dead   c. she shall live   d. an issue of blood twelve years
e. thy faith hath made thee whole

51. St. Matt. 9:23-25
Answer - a. but sleepeth   b. and the maid arose

52. St. Matt. 9:26
Answer - a. all the land

53. St. Matt. 9:28-30
Answer - a. the blind men   b. believe ye that I am able to do this ?   c. touched   d. according to your faith   e. opened

54. St. Matt. 9:32-33
Answer - a. dumb man   b. the dumb spake

55. St. Matt. 10:1
Answer - a. them power   b. heal all manner of sickness and all manner of disease.

56. St. Matt. 10:2-4
Answer - a. Peter   b. Andrew   c. James   d. John   e. Philip   f. Bartholomew   g. Thomas   h. Matthew   I. James   j. Lebbaeus   k. Simon   l. Judas Iscariot

57. St. Matt. 10:7-8
Answer - a. preach   b. freely ye have received, freely give

58. St. Matt. 10:14
Answer - a. shake off the dust of your feet

59. St. Matt. 10:19
Answer - a. no thought   b. be given

60. St. Matt. 10:20
Answer - a. Spirit of your father   b. in you

61. St. Matt. 10:26
Answer - a. nothing covered   b. revealed   c. be known

62. St. Matt. 10:40
Answer - a. receiveth him that sent me

63. St. Matt. 11:1
Answer - a. twelve disciples   b. teach   c. preach

64. St. Matt. 11:2
Answer - a. two of his disciples

65. St. Matt. 7:11
Answer - a. concerning John

66. St. Matt. 11:10
Answer - a. Messenger   b. prepare

67. St. Matt. 11:12
Answer - a. John the Baptist

68. St. Matt. 11:13
Answer - a. Prophesied   b. John

69. St. Matt. 11:30
Answer - a. my burden is light

70. St. Matt. 12:10-13
Answer - a. is it lawful to heal on the Sabbath day?   b. if it fall into a pit on the Sabbath day   c. it is lawful to do well on the Sabbath days   d. stretch forth thine hand

71. St. Matt. 12:30
Answer - a. against me   b. gathered not

72. St. Matt. 12:13
Answer - a. shall be forgiven   b. against the Holy Ghost

73. St. Matt. 12:36
Answer - a. every idle word   b. shall give account thereof

74. St. Matt. 13:3-4
Answer - a. parables   b. fell by the way side

75. St. Matt. 13:4- 8
Answer - a. by the way side, stony places, among thorns   b. good ground

76. St. Matt. 13:23
Answer - a. good ground   b. hundredfold   c. sixty   d. thirty

77. St. Matt. 13:30
Answer - a. gather ye together first the tares

78. St. Matt. 13:36-39
Answer - a. disciples   b. parable   c. Son of man   d. the world   e. kingdom   f. wicked one   g. the devil   h. end of the world   I. the angels

79. St. Matt. 13:49
Answer - a. world   b. sever the wicked from among the just

80. St. Matt. 14:4
Answer - a. not lawful   b. her

81. St. Matt. 14:10
Answer - a. beheaded   b. prison

82. St. Matt. 14:19-21
Answer - a. took the five loaves   b. two fishes   c. disciples   d. twelve basket   e. five thousand men

83. St. Matt. 14:25-31
Answer - a. walking on the sea   b. it is a spirit   c. it is I   d. come   e. come   f. afraid   g. immediately   h. faith

84. St. Matt. 14:36
Answer - a. touch   b. were made perfectly whole

219

85. St. Matt. 15:11
Answer - a. the mouth

86. St. Matt. 15:18-20
Answer - a. proceed out of the mouth   b. from the heart   c. the heart   d. defile a man   e. not

87. St. Matt. 15:28
Answer - a. great is thy faith

88. St. Matt. 16:14-16
Answer - a. John the Baptist   b. Elias   c. Jeremias   d. I AM

89. St. Matt. 16:27
Answer - a. with his angels   b. shall reward every man

90. St. Matt. 17:5
Answer - a. hear ye him

91. St. Matt. 17:22-23
Answer - a. betrayed   b. kill him   c. third day   d. raised again

92. St. Matt. 18:12-13
Answer - a. ninety and nine   b. that

93. St. Matt. 18:19-20
Answer - a. touching any thing   b. two or three   c. midst

94. St. Matt. 18:21-22
Answer - a. seventy times seven

95. St. Matt. 19:24
Answer - a. the eye of a needle   b. kingdom of God

96. St. Matt. 20:16
Answer - a. few chosen

97. St. Matt 20:28
Answer - a. but to minister   b. for many

98. St. Matt. 20:34
Answer - a. compassion   b. followed him

99. St. Matt. 21:1-5
Answer - a. loose them   b. the Lord hast need of them   c. tell ye the daughter of Zion, behold,

100. St. Matt. 21:13-14
Answer - a. cast out   b. table of the moneychangers   c. house of prayer

101. St. Matt. 21:19-22
Answer - a. for ever   b. faith   c. doubt not   d. be thou removed   e. it shall be done   f. believing

102. St. Matt. 22:21
Answer - a. things that are God's

103. St. Matt. 22:25-30
Answer - a. left his wife unto his brother   b. seventh   c. ye do err   d. power of God   e. neither marry nor are given in marriage

104. St. Matt. 22:36-40
Answer - a. the Lord thy God   b. love thy neighbor as thyself   c. hang

105. St. Matt. 23:9
Answer - a. which is in heaven

106. St. Matt. 23:39
Answer - a. blessed is he

107. St. Matt. 24:3
Answer - a. tell us when shall these things be?   b. shall be

108. St. Matt. 24:6
Answer - a. see that ye be not troubled   b. end is not yet come

109. St. Matt. 24:13
Answer - a. the same shall be saved

110. St. Matt. 24:14
Answer - a. all the world   b. and then shall the end come

111. St. Matt. 24:27
Answer - a. east   b. west

112. St. Matt. 24:30
Answer - a. tribes   b. clouds of heaven   c. great glory

113. St. Matt. 24:35
Answer - a. shall not pass away

114. St. Matt. 24:39
Answer - a. coming

115. St. Matt. 24:42
Answer - a. what hour

116. St. Matt. 25:8-11
Answer - a. gone out   b. and buy for yourselves   c. bridegroom come   d. the door was shut   e. Lord, open to us

117. St. Matt. 25:21
Answer - a. faithful   b. ruler   c. the joy of thy lord

118. St. Matt. 25:46
Answer - a. everlasting   b. life eternal

119. St. Matt. 26:1-15

Answer - a. Passover   b. crucified   c. very precious ointment   d. to what purpose is this waste?   e. wheresoever   f. preached   g. be told for a Memorial of her   h. Judas Iscariot   I. covenanted   j. thirty pieces of silver

120. St. Matt. 26:21
Answer - a. shall betray me

121. St. Matt. 26:26-27
Answer - a. blessed it   b. my body   c. gave thanks   d. all of it

122. St. Matt. 26:34
Answer - a. deny me thrice

123. St. Matt. 26:47-49
Answer - a. great multitude   c. whosoever I shall kiss

124. St. Matt. 26:73-75
Answer - a. for thy speech betrayed thee   b. curse and to swear   c. cock crew   d. word of Jesus   e. wept bitterly

125. St. Matt. 27:1-5
Answer - a. death   b. the governor   c. condemned, repented himself   d. the innocent blood   e. hanged himself

126. St. Matt. 27:24
Answer - a. took water, and washed his hands   b. just person

127. St. Matt. 27:45
Answer - a. sixth hour   b. nineth hour

128. St. Matt. 27:46
Answer - a. my God, why hast thou forsaken me?

129. St. Matt. 27:50
Answer - a. yielded up the ghost

130. St. Matt. 28:5-6
Answer - a. seek Jesus   b. he is not here: for he is risen

131. St. Matt. 28:9-10
Answer - a. all hail   b. and there shall they see me

132. St. Matt. 28:16-17
Answer - a. had appointed them   b. but some doubled

133. St. Matt. 28:18-20
Answer - a. in heaven and in earth   b. baptizing   c. whatsoever   d. I am with you always

THE END - ST. MATTHEW

ST. MARK

1. Mark 1:1-2
Answer - a. behold, I send my messenger

2. Mark 1:3
Answer - a. prepare ye the way of the Lord

3. Mark 1:4
Answer - a. repentance for the remission of sins

4. Mark 1:7
Answer - a. one mightier than I   b. stoop down and unloose

5. Mark 1:8
Answer - a. with the Holy Ghost

6. Mark 1:9-14
Answer - a. Jordan   b. heavens opened and the Spirit like a dove   c. thou art my beloved Son   d. wilderness
e. forty days, f. Satan   g. put in prison   h. preaching the gospel

7. Mark 1:15
Answer - a. repent ye and believe the gospel

8. Mark 1:16
Answer - a. Galilee   b. come ye after me   c. to become fishers of men   d. followed him

9. Mark 1:23-26
Answer - a. unclean spirit   b. let us alone   c. I know thee   d. hold thy peace and come out of him   e. had torn him

10. Mark 1:41
Answer - a. compassion   b. I will; be thou clean

11. Mark 1:44
Answer - a. show thyself to the priest   b. for a testimony unto them

12. Mark 2:4-5
Answer - a. uncovered the roof   b. the sick of the palsy lay   c. their faith

13. Mark 2:8-12
Answer - a. preceived in his Spirit   b. hearts   c. Son of man   d. forgive sins   e. take up thy bed   f. immediately

14. Mark 2:17
Answer - a. whole   b. physician   c. sinners to repentance

15. Mark 2:27-28
Answer - a. Sabbath   b. Sabbath   c. Sabbath

16. Mark 3:2
Answer - a. might accuse him

17. Mark 3:5
Answer - a. hardness of their hearts   b. restored whole

18. Mark 3:11
Answer - a. fell down before him

19. Mark 3:14-15
Answer - a. preach   b. power

20. Mark 3:23
Answer - a. satan cast out satan?

21. Mark 3:25
Answer - a. cannot stand

22. Mark 3:29
Answer - a. Holy Ghost   b. eternal damnation

23. Mark 3:35
Answer - a. mother

24. Mark 4:3
Answer - a. sower to sow

25. Mark 4:4-8
Answer - a. parables

26. Mark 4:14
Answer - a. word

27. Mark 4:32
Answer - a. greater   b. great branches   c. shadow

28. Mark 4:39
Answer - a. peace, be still

29. Mark 5:8-9
Answer - a. what is thy name   b. Legion

30. Mark 5:13
Answer - a. entered into the swine   b. choked in the sea

31. Mark 5:19
Answer - a. how great things the Lord hath done, for thee   b. compassion

32. Mark 5:24-34
Answer - a. issue of blood twelve   b. had spent all that she had   c. if I may touch   d. fountain of her blood was dried up   e. healed   f. who touched my clothes?   g. Came and fell down before him   h. thy faith hath made thee whole

33. Mark 6:11
Answer - a. shake off the dust under your feet for a testimony against them

34. Mark 6:16
Answer - a. it is John, whom I beheaded

35. Mark 6:18
Answer - a. thy brother's wife

36. Mark 6:24
Answer - a. the head of John the Baptist

37. Mark 6:28
Answer - a. gave it to her mother

38. Mark 6:38
Answer - a. five and three fishes

39. Mark 6:42
Answer - a. filled

40. Mark 6:44
Answer - a. five thousand men

41. Mark 6:47
Answer - a. midst of the sea

42. Mark 6:49-50
Answer - a. a spirit   b. and immediately he talked with them   c. it is I

43. Mark 7:15
Answer - a. can defile him   b. come out of him

44. Mark 7:16
Answer - a. let him hear

45. Mark 7:37
Answer - a. he maketh both the deaf to hear, and the dumb to speak

46. Mark 8:12
Answer - a. unto this generation

47. Mark 8:23-26
Answer - a. he asked him if he saw aught   b. I see men as trees, walking   b. and saw every man clearly

48. Mark 8:27-30
Answer - a. John the Baptist   b. Elias   c. one of the prophets   d. thou art the Christ

49. Mark 8:34
Answer - a. whosoever will come after me   b. and take up his cross, and follow me

50. Mark 9:2-4
Answer - a. he was transfigured before them   b. Elias   c. Moses   d. talking with Jesus

51. Mark 9:9
Answer - a. Son of Man were risen from the dead

52. Mark 9:17-18
Answer - a. Master   b. which hath a dumb spirit   c. he teareth him   d. and they could not

53. Mark 9:21-29
Answer - a. of a child   b. fire   c. water   d. have compassion on us and help us   e. all things are possible to him that believe   f. help thou mine unbelief   g. thou dumb and deaf spirit   h. enter no more into him I. came out of him   j. could not   k. kind   l. prayer and fasting

54. Mark 9:31-32
Answer - a. rise the third day   b. understood not

55. Mark 9:34
Answer - a. who should be the greatest

56. Mark 9:37
Answer - a. receiveth me   b. but him that sent me

57. Mark 9:40
Answer - a. is on our part

58. Mark 9:44/46/48
Answer - a. not   b. quenched

59. Mark 10:2-3
Answer - a. put away   b. Moses command you?

60. Mark 10:11-12
Answer - a. adultery against her   b. adultery

61. Mark 10:14-17
Answer - a. forbid them not   b. blessed them

62. Mark 10:25
Answer - a. a rich man

63. Mark 10:27
Answer - a. impossible   b. all things are possible

64. Mark 10:37
Answer - a. grant unto us   b. one   c. other

65. Mark 10:45
Answer - a. a ransom for many

66. Mark 10:52
Answer - a. thy faith hath made thee whole

67. Mark 11:21-24
Answer - a. have faith in God   b. shall not doubt in his heart   c. shall have whatsoever he saith   d. believe   e. receive them

68. Mark 12:1
Answer - a. planted a vineyard

69. Mark 12:29-31
Answer - a. heart   b. soul   c. mind   d. strength   e. neighbour

70. Mark 13:10
Answer - a. all nations

71. Mark 13:11
Answer - a take no thought   b. but the Holy Ghost

72. Mark 13:26
Answer - a. power and glory

73. Mark 13:31
Answer - a. shall not pass away

74. Mark 13:32
Answer - a. but the father

75. Mark 13:37
Answer - a. watch

76. Mark 14:6
Answer - a. let her alone,   b. on me

77. Mark 14:13
Answer - a. a pitcher of water

78. Mark 14:15
Answer - a. large upper room

79. Mark 14:18
Answer - a. shall betray me

80. Mark 14:24
Answer - a. new testament

81. Mark 14:26
Answer - a. Mount of Olives

82. Mark 14:30
Answer - a. thou shall deny me thrice

83. Mark 14:38
Answer - a. spirit truly is ready

84. Mark 14:41
Answer - a. sleep on now   b. the hour is come

85. Mark 14:62
Answer - a. right hand of power

86. Mark 15:13
Answer - a. crucify him

87. Mark 15:17
Answer - a. with purple, and plaited a

88. Mark 15:21
Answer - a. to bear his cross

89. Mark 15:22
Answer - a. the place of the skull

90. Mark 15:23
Answer - a. not

91. Mark 15:24
Answer - a. casting lots upon them

92. Mark 15:31
Answer - a. himself he cannot save

93. Mark 15:33
Answer - a. nineth

94. Mark 15:37
Answer - a. loud voice

95. Mark 16:6
Answer - a. he is risen; he is not here

96. Mark 16:9
Answer - a. Mary Magdalene   b. seven devils

97. Mark 16:14
Answer - a. the eleven   b. not them which had seen him after he was risen

98. Mark 16:15-20
Answer - a. preach the gospel to every creature   b. believeth   c. baptized   d. follow them that believe
e. cast out devils   f. new tongues   g. take up serpents   h. deadly thing   I. lay hand on the sick   j.
received up into heaven   k. sat on the right hand of God   l. confirming the word with signs following

THE END - ST. MARK

ST. LUKE

1. St. Luke 1:6-7
Answer - a. blameless   b. was barren

2. St. Luke 1:11-13
Answer - a. shall bear thee a son   b. John

3. St. Luke 1:18-20
Answer - a. I am Gabriel, that stand in the present of God   b. thy shall be dumb and not able to speak   c. believest not   d. remained speechless

4. St. Luke 1:26
Answer - a. the angel Gabriel

5. St. Luke 1:30
Answer - a. favour with God

6. St. Luke 1:31
Answer - a. Jesus

7. St. Luke 1:34
Answer - a. seeing I know not a man?

8. St. Luke 1:35-37
Answer - a. power of the highest   b. the Son of man   c. Elisabeth   d. her old age   e. who was barren   f. nothing shall be impossible

9. St. Luke 1:38
Answer - a. according to thy word

10. St. Luke 1:14
Answer - a. magnify

11. St. Luke 1:57
Answer - a. a son

12. St. Luke 1:63
Answer - a. his name is John

13. St. Luke 1:64
Answer - a. he spake and praised God

14. St. Luke 1:80
Answer - a. showing unto Israel

15. St. Luke 2:7
Answer - a. swaddling clothes

16. St. Luke 2:14
Answer - a. good will toward men

17. St. Luke 2:21
Answer - a. circumcising of the child   b. Jesus   c. conceived in the womb

18. St. Luke 2:29
Answer - a. and the Holy Ghost was upon him   b. see death   c. came by the Spirit   d. blessed God   e. servant depart in peace   f. salvation

19. St. Luke 2:41-41
Answer - a. twelve years old

20. St. Luke 2:43
Answer - a. tarried behind   b. knew not of it

21. St. Luke 2:46
Answer - a. sitting in the midst of the doctors

22. St. Luke 2:49
Answer - a. I must be about my father's business

23. St. Luke 2:52
Answer - a. favour with God and man

24. St. Luke 3:2-3
Answer - a. shall see the salvation of God

25. St. Luke 3:5-6
Answer - a. baptized of him   b. the wrath to come?

26. St. Luke 3:16
Answer - a. but one mightier than I cometh   b. the Holy Ghost and with fire

27. St. Luke 3:20
Answer - a. John in prison

28. St. Luke 3:21-22
Answer - a voice came from heaven   b. in thee I am well pleased

29. St. Luke 3:23
Answer - a. thirty years of age

30. St. Luke 4:1-2
Answer - a. the Holy Ghost   b. forty days   c. eat nothing

31. St. Luke 4:13
Answer - a. he departed from him for a season

32. St. Luke 4:16-21
Answer - a. on the Sabbath day   b. the book of the prophet Esaias   c. the spirit of the Lord is upon me
d. eyes of all them that were in the synagogue   e. fulfilled in your ears

33. St. Luke 4:32
Answer - a. for his word was with power

34. St. Luke 4:36
Answer - a. authority and power

35. St. Luke 4:41
Answer - a. for they knew that he was Christ

36. St. Luke 5:5-6
Answer - a. we have toiled all the night, and have taken nothing   b. a great multitude of fishes

37. St. Luke 5:17
Answer - a. Pharisees and doctors of the law sitting by   b. was present to heal them

38. St. Luke 6:181-19
Answer - a. they were healed   b. sought to touch him

39. St. Luke 6:27-28
Answer - a. do good to them which hate you   b. pray for them

40. St. Luke 6:35
Answer - a. and your reward shall be great

41. St. Luke 6:37
Answer - a. and ye shall be forgiven

42. St. Luke 6:46-48
Answer - a. and heareth my sayings, and doeth them   b. and could not shake it

43. St. Luke 7:13
Answer - a. compassion

44. St. Luke 7:28
Answer - a. John the Baptist

45. St. Luke 7:37-38
Answer - a. and began to wash his feet with tears

46. St. Luke 7:48
Answer - a. forgiven

47. St. Luke 7:50
Answer - a. thy faith

48. St. Luke 8:11
Answer - a. God

49. St. Luke 8:46
Answer - a. virtue is gone out of me

50. St. Luke 8:50
Answer - a. believe only

51. St. Luke 9:1
Answer - a. power and authority

52. St. Luke 9:5
Answer - a. for a testimony against them

53. St. Luke 9:14
Answer - a. fifties in a company

54. St. Luke 9:18-20
Answer - a. but whom say ye that I am

55. St. Luke 9:21
Answer - a. no man that thing

56. St. Luke 9:30
Answer - a. Moses and Elias

57. St. Luke 9:34-35
Answer - a. hear him

58. St. Luke 9:50
Answer - a. not against us is for us

59. St. Luke 9:58
Answer - a. no where to lay his head

60. St. Luke 10:1-3
Answer - a. seventy   b. seventy   c. but the laborers are few   d. I send you forth as lambs among wolves

61. St. Luke 10:17-20
Answer - a. through thy name   b. power   c. power of the enemy   d. your names are written in heaven

62. St. Luke 10:25-26
Answer - a. what shall I do to inherit eternal life?

63. St. Luke 10:36-37
Answer - a. fell among the thieves   b. go and do thou likewise

64. St. Luke 10:42
Answer - a. hath chosen that good part

65. St. Luke 11:1
Answer - a. Lord teach us to pray

66. St. Luke 11:9-10
Answer - a. ask   b. seek   c. knock   d. asketh   e. seeketh   f. knocketh

67. St. Luke 11:23
Answer - a. against   b. scattered

68. St. Luke 11:37-39
Answer - a. sat down to meat   b. first washed before dinner   c. inward part   d. ravening and wickedness

69. St. Luke 12:2
Answer - a. be revealed   b. be known

70. St. Luke 12:10
Answer - a. forgiven him   b. blasphemeth   c. Holy Ghost

71. St. Luke 12:11-12
Answer - a. shall say   b. Holy Ghost shall teach you

72. St. Luke 12:31
Answer - a. be added unto you

73. St. Luke 12:40
Answer - a. when ye think not

74. St. Luke 12:47
Answer - a. beaten with many stripes

75. St. Luke 13:11-13
Answer - a. a spirit of infirmity   b. lift up herself   c. woman, thou are loosed from thine infirmity   d. glorified God

76. St. Luke 13:16
Answer - a. whom Satan hath bound

77. St. Luke 13:28
Answer - a. Abraham and Isaac and Jacob

78. St. Luke 13:30
Answer - a. first which shall be last

79. St. Luke 14:13-14
Answer - a. blessed   b. recompense at the resurrection of the just

80. St. Luke 15:7
Answer - a. sinner that repenteth   b. no repentance

81. St. Luke 15:10
Answer - a. angels of God

82. St. Luke 15:32
Answer - a. dead   b. was lost and is found

83. St. Luke 16:19-24
Answer - a. purple and fine linen   b. every day   c. Lazarus   d. crumbs   e. carried by the angels into Abraham's bosom   f. and in hell he lifted up his eyes   g. dip the tip of his finger in water

84. St. Luke 16:31
Answer - a. Moses and the prophets

85. St. Luke 17:3
Answer - a. forgive him

86. St. Luke 17:12
Answer - a. ten men

87. St. Luke 17:14
Answer - a. they were cleaned

88. St. Luke 17:15
Answer - a. turned back   b. glorified God

89. St. Luke 17:17
Answer - a. but where are the other nine?

90. St. Luke 17:19
Answer - a. faith

91. St. Luke 17:21
Answer - a. is within you

92. St. Luke 17:32
Answer - a. wife

93. St. Luke 18:27
Answer - a. are possible with God

94. St. Luke 18:42
Answer - a. thy faith hath saved thee

95. St. Luke 18:43
Answer - a. glorifying God

96. St. Luke 19:9-10
Answer - a. a son of Abraham   b. that which is lost

97. St. Luke 19:28
Answer - a. ascending up to Jerusalem

98. St. Luke 19:38
Answer - a. peace in heaven, and glory in the hightest

99. St. Luke 19:39
Answer - a. rebuke thy disciples

100. St. Luke 19:40
Answer - a. the stone would immediately cry out

101. St. Luke 20:24-25
Answer - a. Caesar's   b. render therefore unto Caesar   c. God the things which be God

102. St. Luke 20:24-25
Answer - a. whose wife of them is she   b. of this world marry   c. neither marry, nor are given in marriage

103. St. Luke 21:33
Answer - a. my word shall not

104. St. Luke 21:36
Answer - a. pray always   b. accounted worthy

105. St. Luke 22:1-12
Answer - a. the Passover   b. Satan   c. Iscariot   d. twelve   e. covenant   f. Peter and John   g. there shall a man meet you   h. where is the guestchamber   I. furnished

106. St. Luke 22:17-20
Answer - a. I will not drink of the fruit of the vine   b. this is my body   c. this do in remembrance of me
d. new testament in my blood

107. St. Luke 22:31-32
Answer - a. thy faith fail not

108. St. Luke 22:35
Answer - a. nothing

109. St. Luke 22:40
Answer - a. into temptation

110. St. Luke 22:47-48
Answer - a. kiss him   b. with a kiss

111. St. Luke 22:50-51
Answer - a. cut off his right ear   b. and healed him

112. St. Luke 22:61-62
Answer - a. wept bitterly

113. St. Luke 23:1
Answer - a. Pilate

114. St. Luke 23-9
Answer - a. but he answered him nothing

115. St. Luke 23:12
Answer - a. friends together

116. St. Luke 23:16
Answer - a. release him

117. St. Luke 23:21
Answer - a. crucify him

118. St. Luke 23:34
Answer - a. parted his raiment and cast lots

119. St. Luke 23:42-43
Answer - a. today shalt thou be with me in paradise

120. St. Luke 23:46
Answer - a. Father, into thy hands I commend my spirit

121. St. Luke 23:52-53
Answer - a. Jesus   b. wrapped it in linen   c. never

122. St. Luke 23:56
Answer - a. rested the Sabbath day according to the commandment

123. St. Luke 24:2
Answer - a. rolled away

124. St. Luke 24:3
Answer - a. not

125. St. Luke 24:4
Answer - a. shining garments

126. St. Luke 24:6-7
Answer - a. and the third day rise again

127. St. Luke 24:8
Answer - a. words

128. St. Luke 24:12
Answer - a. linen clothes laid by themselves   b. come to pass

129. St. Luke 24:19
Answer - a. Jesus of Nazareth

130. St. Luke 24:23
Answer - a. seen a vision of angels   b. alive

131. St. Luke 24:29
Answer - a. to tarry with them

132. St. Luke 24:31
Answer - a. and they knew him

133. St. Luke 24:38
Answer - a. thoughts arise in your hearts

134. St. Luke 24:39
Answer - a. spirit hath not flesh and bones

135. St. Luke 24:40
Answer - a. his hands and his feet

136. St. Luke 24:45
Answer - a. understand the scriptures

137. St. Luke 24:47-53
Answer - a. beginning at Jerusalem   b. witness   c. Jerusalem, until ye be endued with power from on high   d. Bethany   e. and blessed them   f. carried up into heaven   g. Jerusalem   h. praising and blessing God

THE END - ST. LUKE

ST. JOHN

1. St. John 1:1
Answer - a. word   b. word   c. word

2. St. John 1:3
Answer - a. him   b. him   c. that was made

3. St. John 1:4
Answer - a. life   b. life   c. light of men

4. St. John 1:6
Answer - a. God   b. John

5. St. John 1:7
Answer - a. to bear witness

6. St. John 1:8
Answer - a. of that light

7. St. John 1:13
Answer - a. but of God

8. St. John 1:15
Answer - a. for he was before me

9. St. John 1:32
Answer - a. Spirit descending from heaven

10. St. John 1:34
Answer - a. is the Son of God

11. St. John 1:51
Answer - a. see heaven open   b. ascending and descending

12. St. John 2:2
Answer - a. Marriage

13. St. John 2:3
Answer - a. they have no wine

14. St. John 2:4-5
Answer - a. mine hour is not yet come   b. do it

15. St. John 2:9
Answer - a. that was made wine   b. bridegroom

16.. St. John 2:11
Answer - a. disciples believed on him

17. St. John 2:19
Answer - a. in three days

18. St. John 2:21
Answer - a. body

19. St. John 2:24-25
Answer - a. all men   b. for he knew what was in man

20. St. John 3:4-7
Answer - a. born of water and of the spirit he cannot   b. flesh is flesh   c. Spirit is spirit   d. ye must be born again

21. St. John 3:16
Answer - a. believeth in him

22. St. John 3:19-21
Answer - a. darkness   b. light   c. hateth the light   d. cometh to the light

23. St. John 3:27-28
Answer - a. but that I am sent before him

24. St. John 3:36
Answer - a. but the wrath of God abideth on him

25. St. John 4:6-7
Answer - a. sat thus on the well   b. give me to drink

26. St. John 4:13-14
Answer - a. shall thirst again   b. shall never thirst   c. springing up into everlasting life

27. St. John 4:19
Answer - a. a prophet

28. St. John 4:24
Answer - a. must worship him in spirit and in truth

29. St. John 4:26
Answer - a. am he

30. St. John 4:42
Answer - a. the savior of the world

31. St. John 4:48
Answer - a. not believe

32. St. John 4:49-54
Answer - a. go thy way, thy son liveth   b. believed   c. thy son liveth   d. hour when he began to amend
e. eleventh hour   f. same hour   g. thy son liveth   h. second miracle

33. St. John 5:4-9
Answer - a. troubled the water   b. thirty and eight years   c. wilt thou be made whole?   d. when the
water is troubled   e. rise take up thy bed and walk   f. the Sabbath

34. St. John 5:14
Answer - a. sin no more, lest a worst thing come unto thee

35. St. John 5:22
Answer - a. all judgement unto the Son

36. St. John 5:24
Answer - a. believeth on him that sent me   b. death unto life

37. St. John 5:27
Answer - a. Son of man

38. St. John 5:33
Answer - a. bare witness

39. St. John 5:46
Answer - a. for he wrote of me

40. St. John 6:9
Answer - among so many?

41. St. John 6:13
Answer - a. over and above

42. St. John 6:19-20
Answer - a. walking on the sea   b. be not afraid

43. St. John 6:35
Answer - a. shall never hunger   b. shall never thirst

44. St. John 6:47
Answer - a. everlasting life

45. St. John 6:48
Answer - a. that

46. St. John 6:54
Answer - a. I will raise him up

47. St. John 6:63
Answer - a. they are spirit

48. St. John 6:70
Answer - a. one of you is a devil

49. St. John 7:16
Answer - a. but his that sent me

50. St. John 7:26
Answer - a. this is the very Christ

51. St. John 7:28-29
Answer - a. I know him; for I am from him

52. St. John 7:37-38
Answer - a. belly shall flow rivers of living water

53. St. John 8:7-8
Answer - a. let him first cast a stone at her

54. St. John 8:11
Answer - a. neither do I condemn thee, go and sin no more

55. St. John 8:12
Answer - a. darkness   b. light of life

56. St. John 8:19
Answer - a. ye should have known my Father also

57. St. John 8:31-32
Answer - a. and the truth shall make you free

58. St. John 8:56
Answer - a. and he saw it, and was glad

59. St. John 8:58
Answer - a. before Abraham was, I AM

60. St. John 9:6
Answer - a. he spat on the ground   b. anointed the eyes

61. St. John 9:11
Answer - a. and I received sight

62. St. John 9:21
Answer - a. he is of age, ask him, he shall speak for himself

63. St. John 10:27-30
Answer - a. and they follow me   b. pluck them out of my hand   c. no man is able   d. one

64. St. John 10:37-38
Answer - a. believe the works   b. Father is in me, and I in him

65. St. John 11:14-15
Answer - a. to the intent you may believe

66. St. John 11:17
Answer - a. laid in the grave four days already

67. St. John 11:24-26
Answer - a. I am the resurrection   b. yet shall he live   c. shall never die

68. St. John 11:33
Answer - a. he groaned in the spirit, and was troubled

69. St. John 10:35
Answer - a. (no response) (ALSO, SHORTEST VERSE IN THE BIBLE !!)

70. St. John 11:41-44
Answer - a. but because of the people   b. believe   c. Lazarus, come forth   d. loose him and let him go

71. St. John 12:28-32
Answer - a. said that it thundered   b. but for your sakes   c. will draw all men unto me

72. St. John 13:1-2
Answer - a. the devil   b. heart of Judas Iscariot   c. to betray him

73. St. John 13:17
Answer - a. If ye do them

74. St. John 13:21
Answer - a. shall betray me

75. St. John 13:34
Answer - a. that ye also love one another

76. St. John 14:1
Answer - a. believe also in me

77. St. John 14:6
Answer - a. no man cometh unto the Father, but by me

78. St. John 14:13-16
Answer - a. that will I do   b. I will do it   c. keep my commandments d. Comforter

79. St. John 14:26
Answer - a. Holy Ghost   b. bring all things to your remembrance

80. St. John 15:5
Answer - a. ye can do nothing

81. St. John 15:7
Answer - a. it shall be done unto you

82. St. John 15:11
Answer - a. joy   b. might be full

83. St. John 15:27
Answer - a. from the beginning

84. St. John 16:7
Answer - a. the Comforter will not come unto you

85. St. John 16:13
Answer - a. shall not speak of himself   b. that shall he speak

86. St. John 16:20
Answer - a. but your sorrow shall be turned into joy

87. St. John 16:21
Answer - a. she remembered no more the anguish

88. St. John 16:23
Answer - a. whatsoever   b. in my name

89. St. John 16:26
Answer - a. that I will pray

90. St. John 16:27
Answer - a. believed   b. out from God

91. St. John 17:2-4
Answer - a. only true God and Jesus Christ,   b. glorified   c. finished the work   d. me to do

92. St. John 17:7
Answer - a. are of thee

93. St. John 17:9
Answer - a. for they are thine

94. St. John 17:12
Answer - a. and none of them is lost

95. St. John 17:14
Answer - a. because they are not of the world

96. St. John 17:17
Answer - a. thy word is truth

97. St. John 17:26
Answer - a. and I in them

98. St. John 18:7-9
Answer - a. Jesus of Nazareth   b. I am he   c. have I lost none

99. St. John 18:20
Answer - a. and in secret have I said nothing

100. St. John 18:27
Answer - a. immediately

101. St. John 18:33
Answer - a. judgement hall again   b. king of the Jews

102. St. John 18:38
Answer - a. I find in him no fault at all

103. St. John 19:2
Answer - a.   a purple role

104. St. John 19:11
Answer - a. except it were given thee from above   b. the greater sin

105. St. John 19:30
Answer - a. it is finished

106. St. John 19:33-34
Answer - a. they brake not his legs   b. blood and water

107. St. John 19:36:37
Answer - a. a bone of him shall not be broken

108. St. John 20:7
Answer - a. in a place by itself

109. St. John 20:11-14
Answer - a. two angels in white,   b. head   c. feet   d taken away my Lord   e. and saw Jesus standing

110. St. John 20:17
Answer - a. touch me not   b. I ascend unto my Father   c. my God

111. St. John 20:20
Answer - a. his hands and his side

112. St. John 20:22
Answer - a. he breathed on them   b. the Holy Ghost

113. St. John 20:24
Answer - a. Jesus came

114. St. John 20:29
Answer - a. Thomas   b. not seen, and yet have believed

115. St. John 21:14
Answer - a. was risen from the dead

116. St. John 21:22
Answer - a. follow me

117. St. John 21:25
Answer - a. which Jesus did   b. the world itself   c. the books that should be written.

THE END - ST. JOHN

THE ACTS

1. Acts 1:4-5
Answer - a. they should not depart from Jerusalem, but wait   b. with the Holy Ghost

2. Acts 1:8-11
Answer - a. Jerusalem   b. Judaea   c. Samaria   d. receive him out of their sight   e. shall so come in like manner

3. Acts 1:24
Answer - a. all men   b. two

4. Acts 1:26
Answer - a. Matthias   b. eleven apostles

5. Acts 2:1
Answer - a. one accord in one place

6. Acts 2:2
Answer - a. rushing mighty wind

7. Acts 2:4
Answer - a. Holy Ghost   b. other tongues

8. Acts 2:13
Answer - a. wine

9. Acts 2:17
Answer - a. I will pour out of my Spirit upon all flesh   b. shall prophesy   c. visions   d. dream dreams

10. Acts 2:21
Answer - a. shall be saved

11. Acts 2:38
Answer - a. gift of the Holy Ghost

12. Acts 2:40
Answer - a. untoward generation

13. Acts 2:41
Answer - a. baptized   b. three thousand souls

14. Acts 2:44
Answer - a. common

15. Acts 3:2
Answer - a. beautiful

16. Acts 3:6-7
Answer - a. but such as I have give I thee   b. rise up and walk   c. received strength

17. Acts 3:14-16
Answer - a. through faith in his name   b. the faith

18. Acts 3:25
Answer - a. unto Abraham   b. be blessed

19. Acts 4:3
Answer - a. until the next day

20. Acts 4:13
Answer - a. being with Jesus

21. Acts 4:18
Answer - a. in the name of Jesus

22. Acts 4:21
Answer - a. for all men glorified God

23. Acts 4:24
Answer - a. to God with one accord   b. heaven and earth and the sea

24. Acts 4:35
Answer - a. distribution   b. according as he had need

25. Acts 5:1-3
Answer - a. kept back part   b. and laid it at the apostle's feet   c. to lie to the Holy Ghost

26. Acts 5:5
Answer - a. gave up the ghost

27. Acts 5:7
Answer - a. came in

28. Acts 5:9-10
Answer - a. the Spirit of the Lord   b. are at the door   c. yielded up the ghost   d. buried her by her husband

29. Acts 5:15
Answer - a. shadow of Peter passing by

30. Acts 5:18-20
Answer - a. prison   b. opened the prison doors

31. Acts 5:29
Answer - a. we ought to obey God rather than man

32. Acts 5:32
Answer - a. the Holy Ghost   b. that obey him

33. Acts 5:42
Answer - a. Jesus Christ

34. Acts 6:8
Answer - a. among the people

35. Acts 6:10
Answer - a. wisdom and the spirit

36. Acts 6:15
Answer - a. the face of an angel

37. Acts 7:8
Answer - a. Abraham begat Isaac   b. Jacob   c. the twelve Patriarch

38. Acts 7:9
Answer - a. but God was with him

39. Acts 7:20-21
Answer - a. three months   b. Pharaoh's daughter   c. own son

40. Acts 7:23
Answer - a. children of Israel

41. Acts 7:28-33
Answer - a. fled   b. Madian   c. two sons   d. flame of fire in a bush   e. the voice of the Lord came unto him   f. put off thy shoes from thy feet; for the place where thou standest is holy ground

42. Acts 7:55
Answer - a. Jesus standing on the right hand of God

43. Acts 7:58
Answer - a. stoned him   b. whose name was Saul

44. Acts 7:59-60
Answer - a. Lord lay not this sin to their charge

45. Acts 8:1
Answer - a. a great persecution against the church   b. Judaea and Samaria

46. Acts 8:3
Answer - a. and haling men and women

47. Acts 8:9
Answer - a. great one

246

48. Acts 8:18
Answer - a. offered them money

49. Acts 8:20
Answer - a. perish   b. gift of God

50. Acts 8:22
Answer - a. thought of thine heart

51. Acts 8:29
Answer - a. chariot

52. Acts 8:37-39
Answer - a. I believe that Jesus Christ is the son of God   b. stand still   c. baptized him   d. the spirit of the Lord caught away Philip

53. Acts 9:3-4
Answer - a. a light from heaven   b. Saul, why persecutest me?

54. Acts 9:9
Answer - a. without sight

55. Acts 9:10
Answer - a. Damarcus named Ananias   b. I am here Lord

56. Acts 9:15
Answer - for he is a chosen vessel unto me

57. Acts 9:18
Answer - a. scales   b. sight   c. baptized

58. Acts 9:20
Answer - a. Son of God

59. Acts 9:23
Answer - a. counsel to kill him

60. Acts 9:25
Answer - a. wall in a basket

61. Acts 9:27
Answer - a. preached boldly   b. name of Jesus

62. Acts 9:40
Answer - a. she sat up

63. Acts 10:3-4
Answer - a. an angel of God coming in to him   b. thy prayers and thine alms are come up for a memorial before God

64. Acts 10:8
Answer - them to Joppa

65. Acts 10:10
Answer - a. he fell into a trance

66. Acts 10:15
Answer - a. that call not thou common

67. Acts 10:1920
Answer - a. doubting nothing; for I have sent them

68. Acts 10:26
Answer - a. I myself also am a man

69. Acts 10:35
Answer - a. with him

70. Act 10:43-44
Answer - a. shall receive remission of sins   b. the Holy Ghost

71. Acts 10:47
Answer - a. the Holy Ghost as well as we?

72. Acts 11:15-19
Answer - a. who believed on the Lord Jesus Christ   b. then has God also to the Gentiles granted repentance unto life   c. Stephen   d. preaching the word to none but unto the Jews only

73. Acts 12:2
Answer - a. sword

74. Acts 12:5
Answer - a. without ceasing   b. God for him

75. Acts 12:6
Answer - a. Peter was sleeping

76. Acts 12:7
Answer - a. arise up quickly and his chains fell off from his hands

77. Acts 12:11
Answer - a. sent his angel   b. expectation

78. Acts 12:21-23
Answer - a. the angel of the Lord   b. and he was eaten of worms, and

79. Acts 13:6
Answer - a. a false prophet   b. Bar-jesus

80. Acts 13:9
Answer - a. set his eyes on him

81. Acts 13:11
Answer - a. not seeing the sun for a season   b. a mist and a darkness   c. lead him by the hand

82. Acts 13:16
Answer - a. give audience

83. Acts 13:22
Answer - a. which shall fulfill all my will

84. Acts 13:25
Answer - a. whose shoes of his feet I am not worthy to loose

85. Acts 13:39
Answer - a. by the law of Moses

86. Acts 13:44-45
Answer - a. God   b. envy   c. Paul

87. Acts 13:51
Answer - a. against them

88. Acts 14:2
Answer - a. made their minds evil

89. Acts 14:6-10
Answer - a. preached the gospel   b. who never had walked   c. faith to be healed   d. and he leaped and walked

90. Acts 14:19
Answer - a. stoned Paul   b. supposing he had been dead

91. Acts 14:23
Answer - a. commended them to the Lord

92. Acts 15:8-9
Answer - a. purifying their hearts by faith

93. Acts 15:23
Answer - a. the apostles and elders and brethren send greeting

94. Acts 15:28-29
Answer - a. no greater burden than these necessary things

95. Acts 15:39-40
Answer - a. they departed asunder one from the other   b. Silas and departed

96. Acts 16:17-18
Answer - a. but Paul, being grieved, turned and said to the spirit

97. Acts 16:23
Answer - a. they cast them into prison

98. Acts 16:25
Answer - a. and the prisoners heard them

99. Acts 16:28
Answer - a. for we are all here

100. Acts 16:39
Answer - a. out of the city

101. Acts 17:14
Answer - a. but Silas and Timotheus abode there still

102. Acts 17:16
Answer - a. wholly given to idolatry

103. Acts 17:23-24
Answer - a. to the unknown God   b. all things therein   c. not in

104. Acts 17:28
Answer - a. for we are also his offspring

105. Acts 17:30
Answer - a. all men every where to repent

106. Acts 17:33
Answer - a. departed

107. Acts 18:9-10
Answer - a. by a vision   b. hold not thy peace

108. Acts 18:18
Answer - a. Priscilla and Aquila   b. for he had a vow

109. Acts 18:26
Answer - a. they took him unto them   b. God more perfectly

110. Acts 19:4-7
Answer - a. come after him,   b. in the name of Lord Jesus   c. the Holy Ghost came upon them   d. twelve

111. Acts 19:15-16
Answer - a. but who are ye?   b. naked and wounded

112. Acts 19:18
Answer - a. their deeds

113. Acts 19:23
Answer - a. assembly was confused

114. Acts 19:40-41
Answer - a. he dismissed the assembly

115. Acts 20:9-10
Answer - a. fell down from the third loft   b. for his life is in him

116. Acts 20:25-28
Answer - a. shall see my face no more   b. blood of all men   c. the Holy Ghost hath made you overseers
d. with his own blood

117. Acts 20:35
Answer - a. blessed to give than to receive

118. Acts 20:36-38
Answer - a. fell on Paul's neck   b. no more

119. Acts 21:4
Answer - a. should not

120. Acts 21:13
Answer - a. to die at Jerusalem

121. Acts 21:27
Answer - a. in the temple   b. laid hands on him

122. Acts 21:31
Answer - a. all Jerusalem was in an uproar

123. Acts 21:40 and 22:1
Answer - a. he spake unto them in the Hebrew tongue   b. my defense

124. Acts 22:3
Answer - a. taught according   b. law of the fathers

125. Acts 22:8
Answer - a. whom thou persecutes

126. Acts 22:10
Answer - a. all things which are appointed for thee to do

127. Acts 22:13
Answer - a. same hour I looked up upon him

128. Acts 22:16
Answer - a. wash away thy sins,

129. Acts 22:20
Answer - a. Stephen was shed, I also was standing by,

130. Acts 23:7
Answer - a. and the multitude was divided

131. Acts 23:9
Answer - a. we find no evil in this man   b. let us not fight against God

251

132. Acts 23:22
Answer - a. and charged him   b. these things to me

133. Acts 24:14-16
Answer - a. there shall be a resurrection of the dead, both of the just and unjust   b. void of offence

134. Acts 24:25
Answer - a. go thy way for this time;   b. I will call for thee

135. Acts 25:10
Answer - a. to the Jews have I done no wrong

136. Acts 25:12
Answer - a. unto Caesar shalt thou go

137. Acts 25:25
Answer - a. I have determined to send him

138. Acts 25:27
Answer - a. to send a prisoner

139. Acts 26:13
Answer - a. a light from heaven above the brightness of the sun

140. Acts 26:16
Answer - a. to make thee a minister and a witness

141. Acts 26:18
Answer - a. darkness to light   b. by faith that is in me

142. Acts 26:28
Answer - a. me to be a christian

143. Acts 26:31
Answer - a. nothing worthy of death or of bonds

144. Acts 27:10
Answer - a. will be with hurt and much damage

145. Acts 27:14
Answer - a. Euroclydon

146. Acts 27:21
Answer - a. hearkened unto me

147. Acts 27:44
Answer - a. escaped all safe to land

148. Acts 28:3
Answer - a. viper

149. Acts 28:5
Answer - a. no harm

150. Acts 28:18
Answer - a. no cause of death in me

151. Acts 28:24
Answer - a. and some believed not

152. Acts 28:30-31
Answer - a. Preaching the kingdom of God and teaching those things which concern

THE END - THE ACTS

ESSAY - THE OLD TESTAMENT

The Book of Genesis (6Q)

1. List each day 1-7, and describe what the Lord God did each day. Explain the difference between the tree of knowledge of good and evil and the tree of live.

2. Explain the circumstances around Abel's killing and what was the vengeance of God to Cain?

3. Give a vivid description of the Ark and how many peoples were saved. How many days did the water prevail upon the earth?

4. Who was Hagar and Ishmael? What was Ishmael's blessings?

5. Who was Jacob and Esau? Why did Esau hate Jacob? What were the circumstances regarding Jacob's wives, Leah and Rachel? Why did Jacob flee from Laban?

6. Who was Joseph's parents? Give accounts of Joseph's life from the time he was seventeen until his death.

The Book of Exodus (3Q)

1. Moses was a Hebrew, explain why he was reared by the Egyptian?

2. List at least five (5) of the plagues that was upon Pharaoh and his people.

3. List the Ten commandments

The Book of Leviticus (3Q)

1. Nabad and Abihu, the sons of Aaron, died before the Lord. Why? What did Moses say and what did Aaron say?

2. List some of the blessings for obedience and list some of the punishments for disobedience. (chapter 26)

3. What portion of tithes is holy unto the Lord?

The Book of Numbers (5Q)

1. What tribe was in charge over the tabernacle of testimony and all the vessels thereof?

2. What are the three vows of a Nazarite?

3. Why was the anger of the Lord kindled against Miriam and Aaron? What happened to Miriam?

4. The tithes of the Children of Israel, the Lord gave to the Levities. What were commanded by the Lord to the Levities and what part should be their tithes?

5. Moses saw the promised land from what mountain? Why didn't Moses make it to the promised land? Who was given charge over the Children of Israel to lead them to the promised land?

The Book of Deuteronomy (3Q)

1. Moses said unto them, Hear O'Isreal, the statutes and judgments which I speak into your ears this day, that ye may learn them, and keep them, and do them. The Lord our God made a Covenant with us in Horeb. What was that Covenant called? List at least five of them.

2. List the blessings of obedience. Read again the curses of disobedience.

3. Where did Moses die and where was he buried? How long did he live? Who had the charge of leading the Children of Israel to the promised land? How long did the Children of Israel wept for Moses?

THE END – ESSAY – THE OLD TESTAMENT

ESSAY - THE NEW TESTAMENT

The Book of St. Matthew (5Q)

1. Who was John the Baptist? What clothing did he wear and what was his meat?

2. Explain the parable of the sower.

3. What defiles a man?

4. Jesus healed many. Matthew 9:18-22, Matthew 9:27-30 and Matthew 14:25-32 are three different healings. What did each of these healings have in common?

5. After the resurrection, what was the great commission given to the eleven disciples in Galilee and why is there only eleven disciples instead of twelve at this time?

The Book of St. Mark (5Q)

1. List the twelve ordained disciples.

2. List the sin that is in danger of eternal damnation because it cannot be forgiven.

3. The disciples had the power to cast out devils, however, they were unable to heal this demoniac boy which had a dumb spirit. Why?

4. Who betrayed Jesus and why? Who denied Jesus and how many times were he denied?

5. What color was Jesus clothed in after he was led away to be crucified?

The Book of St. Luke (6Q)

1. While Zacharias was standing in the altar of incense, an angel spake with him. Who was the angel; what was the message and the results of Zacharias' unbelief?

2. Describe the surrounding events of the birth of Jesus.

3. What was written in the book of the Prophet Esaias when Jesus opened it?

4. Jesus called his twelve disciples together and gave them power and authority over all devils, and to cure diseases. What was his commission to them at that gathering?

5. Describe the parable of the lost son.

6. Jesus opened their understanding, that they might understand the scriptures, why did he want them to tarry in Jerusalem?

The Book of St. John (7Q)

1. John the Baptist was sent from God to bear witness of Jesus. What was his message?

2. The scribes and Pharisees brought unto Jesus a woman taken in adultery, the very act. How did Jesus respond to the Pharisees?

3. What is the shortest verse in the Bible?

4. How did Jesus identify the disciple that was going to betray him?

5. In reference to the Crucifixion: what was the place called that they took Jesus? Who wrote the title on the cross and what did it say? How many languages were the title written in and name the languages.

6. After they had crucified Jesus, they took his garments and made four parts. What was the deciding factor that made the soldiers cast lot for Jesus' coat?

7. Which of the disciples was missing when Jesus returned after the resurrection? What did Jesus do to encourage him to have faith and to believe?

The Book of Acts (8Q)

1. Under what circumstances were Saul converted? What did Saul's name change to after the conversion?

2. Explain Peter's trance and what was his vision?

3. Peter was sleeping while the church prayed for him. And when he came to himself, what did he realize?

4. How and why did Herod die?

5. Explain the separation of Paul and Barnabas, and who did Paul choose to teach and preach with him, after the separation?

6. Paul was "long winded" when he preached. What happened to Eutychus during one of these sessions?

7. On the island called Melita, Paul was bitten by a viper. What harm came to him and how did the Barbarians react to this incident?

8. Upon Paul's arrival in Rome, he called the chief of the Jews together. And when they had appointed him a day to preach/teach, what were the turn of events?

THE END – ESSAY – THE NEW TESTAMENT

ANSWERS ONLY TO THE OLD TESTAMENT ESSAYS (AO)

GENESIS - SIX (6) ESSAY AO

1. GENESIS CHAPTERS 1- 3

2. GENESIS CHAPTER 4

3. GENESIS 6:3-16 AND GENESIS 7:24

4. GENESIS 16: 1 AND 4   GENESIS 16:10-11

5. GENESIS 25: 24-26

    GENESIS 27: 36 AND 41

    GENESIS 29: 1-26

    GENESIS 31: 1-20

6. GENESIS 30: 23-24

    GENESIS CHAPTER 37 TO CHAPTER 50

EXODUS – THREE (3) ESSAY AO

1. EXODUS 2:5-6

2. (1) ROD TO A SERPENT   (2) RIVER WATER BECAME BLOOD

    (3) FROGS   (4) LICE   (5) SWARMS OF FLIES   (6) BOILS

    (7) ASHES BECOME DUST   (8) GRIEVOUS RAIL/HAIL

    (9) LOCUSTS   (10) PLAGUE OF DARKNESS

3. EXODUS 20:3-17

LEVITICUS – THREE (3) ESSAY AO

1. LEVITICUS 10:1-3

2. LEVITICUS CHAPTER 26

3. LEVITICUS 27:32

NUMBERS – FIVE (5) AO

1. NUMBERS 1:53

2. NUMBERS CHAPTER 6

3. NUMBERS CHAPTER 12

4. NUMBERS 18:24-26

5. NUMBERS 27:12-23

DEUTERONOMY – TRREE (3) AO

1. DEUTERONOMY 5:1-22

2. DEUTERONOMY CHAPTER 28

3. DEUTERONOMY 34:4-9

THE END – AO – OLD TESTAMENT

THE ANSWERS ONLY TO THE NEW TESTAMENT ESSAYS (AO)

ST. MATTHEW - FIVE (5) ESSAY AO

1. MATTHEW CHAPTER 3

2. MATTHEW 13:18-30

3. MATTHEW 15:13-20

4. MATTHEW 9:18-22

   MATTHEWS 9;27-30

   MATTHEW 14:25-32

5. MATTHEW 28:16-20

ST. MARK - FIVE (5) ESSAY AO

1. MARK 3:14-18

2. MARK 3:29

3. MARK 9:29

4. MARK 14:43-44

   MARK 14:68

   MARK 14:70-71

5. MARK 15:17

ST. LUKE - SIX (6) ESSAY AO

1. LUKE 1:11

   LUKE 1:19-20

2. LUKE 2:7-16

3. LUKE 4:17-19

4. LUKE 9:1-5

5. LUKE 15:11-32

6. LUKE 24: 45-49

ST. JOHN - SEVEN (7) ESSAY AO

1. JOHN 1:14-23

2. JOHN 8:6-18

3. JOHN 11:35

4. JOHN 13:21-27

5. JOHN 19:17-20

6. JOHN 19:23-24

7. JOHN 20:24

   JOHN 20:27

THE ACTS - EIGHT (8) ESSAY AO

1. ACTS 9:1-21

   ACTS 13:9

2. ACTS 11:5-9

3. ACTS 12:11

4. ACTS 12:23

5. ACTS 15:35-40

6. ACTS 20:9-12

7. ACTS 28:3-6

8. ACTS 28:23-31

THE END – ESSAY AO – THE NEW TESTAMENT